Successful Business Writing

How to Write Effective Letters, Proposals, Résumés, and Speeches

Lassor A. Blumenthal

A PERIGEE BOOK

To Adam, with Love

Perigee Books
are published by
The Putnam Publishing Group
200 Madison Avenue
New York, NY 10016

Library of Congress Cataloging in Publication Data

Blumenthal, Lassor A.
    Successful business writing.

    Includes index.   ng
    1. Commercial correspondence.   I. Title.
HF5726.B58   1985   651.7′5   84-18970
ISBN 0-399-51146-6

Printed in the United States of America

10

Contents

1. How to Organize Your Ideas

SUCCESSFUL BUSINESSES USUALLY *look* like successful businesses. In a successful store, the merchandise is well organized so that customers can find what they want easily. The store's interior looks inviting, and people enjoy coming to it.

Successful business letters are very much like successful stores. They're well organized and they look good.

Interestingly enough, the difference between a good letter and a poor one is usually slight. If you feel that writing good letters is a skill that will be difficult for you to master, you're probably underestimating yourself. Usually, it takes only a little careful thought to make a poor letter into a good one.

Here's an example. An electrical repair shop billed a customer $9 for fixing a tape recorder. The customer objected to the charge because the recorder was still under warranty. The shop sent the following explanation.

> Mrs. Marder:
> The charge for the recorder was not in warrenty. The charge was for the labor, this is not covered by warrenty after 90 days. That is why the charge. The co. will not send the unit back until the repair is paid for, that is just there way of doing business.
>
> Thank you for your understanding.
> Service Dept.

Here's one way the letter might have been made clearer:

> Dear Mrs. Marder:
> The charge on your recorder was for the labor. This is not covered by warranty after 90 days.
>
> The company will be glad to send the unit back as soon as the repair is paid for.
>
> Thank you for your understanding.
> Service Department

What are the major differences between the two letters? The answers will provide us with some of the basic principles of a well-organized business letter.

―――――――――――― **HELPFUL HINTS** ――――――――――――

Make sure your spelling is correct. Check any words you're not sure of.

1. *Spelling.* A number of words were incorrectly spelled in the first letter, such as "warranty" and "their." These are common errors.

Keep your sentences simple: one idea to one sentence.

2. *Sentence structure.* When you put more than one thought into a sentence, it becomes hard to read. That's why the original sentence, "The charge was for the labor, this is not covered by warrenty after 90 days," was changed to two separate sentences: "The charge on your recorder was for labor. This is not covered by warranty after 90 days."

Keep your paragraphs short: as short as one sentence, if you prefer. As a general rule, keep them less than four lines long.

3. *Paragraphing.* Short paragraphs are usually easier to understand than long ones. One reason the second letter is easier to understand is that it's broken into three short paragraphs.

Eliminate information that isn't necessary to understand your message. As a general rule, shorter letters are better letters.

4. *Unnecessary information.* The first letter contained information that the reader didn't need in order to understand the message. The second letter eliminated phrases such as, "that is just there way of doing business." An excess of information is like static on the radio: it tends to interfere with your basic message.

Keep your language positive: when it's possible, change a negative idea to a positive idea.

5. *Replacing negatives with positives.* In the first letter, there were two negative ideas: "labor . . . is not covered" and "The co. will not send the unit back . . ." The revised letter changed the second negative to a positive. Why? Because a negative idea says "no" to a customer. Positive ideas say "yes" to the customer: they invite the customer to continue doing business.

Reread your letters once before signing them.

6. *Checking the finished letter.* Before signing your name to a letter, read it over to see if you can spot any errors. If the repair shop's letter writer had done so, he might have caught some of the errors and corrected them.

Let's review the six basic suggestions:

1. Make sure your spelling is correct.
2. Keep your sentences confined to one idea.
3. Use short paragraphs.
4. Eliminate unnecessary information.
5. Replace negatives with positives when possible.
6. Reread your letters before you sign them.

These principles will clear up many of the common errors that letter writers make. But one major problem remains: how do you put a good letter together?

How do you begin? Where do you go after you've begun? And when do you end? You can take a hint from the King in *Alice in Wonderland,* who said, "Begin at the beginning and go on until you come to the end. Then stop."

HOW TO ORGANIZE YOUR LETTER

Let's see how the King's advice applies to business letter writing.
First, get a piece of scratch paper and list the important ideas you want to get across. Here's an example.

Suppose a supplier has sent you some material that's below quality and which you can't use. You want to send him a letter stating that you're going to return it. You also want credit for the defective material, and you want a fresh shipment right away. Furthermore, you want to warn him that if he ships another lot like that one, you'll start buying from another supplier. In addition, you're thinking about buying the material in different colors, and you're wondering whether he can supply them. Also, you plan on taking a trip shortly and may visit his town; you'd like to see his plant while you're there. There is also a small credit due you from an old invoice; you want your account cleared up.

How do you put all this in a letter? How do you decide what to begin with? What to put next? And so on.

To answer these questions, you can begin by making a single decision: Do you want your letter to talk about one subject or more than one?

As a general rule, the more subjects you discuss, the less impact each one will have. So, if you're really angry about the below-quality material, it might be wise to devote your entire letter to it.

If this is the case, list on your scratch paper the main things you want to talk about:
Poor quality material
Returning it
Demand credit
May get another supplier
Want replacement material immediately

Now, look at your list and decide which of those items is the most important. Number that "1." Number the second most important item "2," and so on.

Your list might now look like this:
2. Poor quality material
1. Returning it
3. Demand credit
5. May get another supplier
4. Want replacement material immediately

Now, you're ready to write your letter. Begin with your No. 1 idea—returning the material—and work your way through to No. 5—getting another supplier. Your letter might read:

Dear Mr. Mansor:
I'm returning the last shipment of material you sent me.
The quality was poor. It was too thin, and the color was wrong.

Please give me full credit of $200 for the returned shipment.

I need a replacement for this order: please send it immediately.

I hope that you will be able to maintain quality in your products. Otherwise, I'll have to look for another supplier.

Sincerely,

This, of course, is only one of many ways you might organize the paragraphs in your letter. The main point is that, by making a brief outline first, you put yourself in control of what you want to say.

Suppose you decide to write about all the things on your mind rather than only the defective shipment. How could you organize that letter clearly and quickly? By following exactly the same procedure: that is, by listing all the things you want to talk about, then numbering them in order of their importance. Your list might look like this:

2. Poor quality material
1. Returning it
3. Demand credit
5. May get another supplier
4. Want replacement material immediately
7. Different colors available?
8. Visit plant
6. Clear up old invoice

When you begin your letter, your first sentence will state that you're going to talk about several different important things. This will act like a red flag, telling the reader to pay close attention to the entire message. Your letter might read like this:

Dear Mr. Mansor:

There are several important matters I want to discuss in this letter.

First, I'm returning the last shipment of material you sent me.

The quality was poor. The material was too thin, and the color was wrong.

Please give me full credit of $200 for the returned shipment.

I will also need a replacement for this order: please send it to me without further delay.

I hope that you will be able to maintain quality in your products. Otherwise, I'll have to look for another supplier.

Second, I'd like to discuss your invoice No. 2356, for $27.37. As we've agreed in the past, this amount has been paid. Please correct your records and eliminate this charge from my statements.

Third, I'd like to know if you can supply your material in gold and silver colors. If so, what would you charge?

Finally, I plan to be in Kansas City on January 15, and I'd like to take a tour of your plant in the early afternoon, if that will be convenient.

I'll look forward to hearing from you.

Sincerely,

John B. Williams

───────────────── **HELPFUL HINT** ─────────────────

Notice that the important ideas were introduced by the words "First," "Second," etc. This is a simple way to indicate that you're starting a new thought and a good way to make each of your points stand out clearly.

A DIFFERENT TECHNIQUE

If you find it difficult to make lists, the previous suggestions about list making will be of little help to you. A different method may be more useful in helping you construct a good letter.

When you're ready to write, get a sheet of scratch paper and put down the first idea that comes into your head. Don't worry about whether or not it makes sense. And, once you've written it, don't try to correct it.

Now, write down the second idea that comes to mind. If it's similar to the first idea, that's perfectly all right. Don't bother correcting it yet.

Instead, write down the next idea that comes into your head. And keep on writing until you've put down all the things you want to say.

At that point, you're ready to rewrite your letter. You may find that there's very little you want to change. Or, you may find that you've written far too much. But now your task is relatively easy, because most of what you want to say is already on the paper in front of you.

————————————— HELPFUL HINT —————————————

If you have trouble writing when you're faced with a large sheet of blank paper, try writing on a small sheet—say 3 x 5 inches. You may find it eliminates the fear of having to fill up the huge expanse of empty space.

ENDING YOUR LETTER EFFECTIVELY

How can you end your letter effectively? Keep in mind this thought: *a good ending tells your reader what you want him or her to do as a result of your letter.*

If you're sending a sales letter, a good ending paragraph will urge the recipient to buy now.

> If you send in the enclosed card today, we know you'll be delighted with the beautiful assortment you'll receive.

> If you send us your order immediately, you'll be guaranteed a bonus set of silver spoons.

If you're sending a collection letter, the last paragraph should urge payment.

> If you'll put your check in the mail today, we'll be able to restore your credit rating to its former high standing.

> Please send us the amount you owe today.

If you're seeking information, the last paragraph might express your appreciation or ask for a quick response.

> I'll be very grateful if you can send the information quickly.

> If you do not have this information, I'd be grateful if you could suggest another source for it.

BETTER OPENINGS AND CLOSINGS

While the suggestions made in the previous paragraphs give you the basic elements involved in any good business letter, there are a few additional points that are useful to remember. They concern the way you open your letter and the way you end it.

First, the openings. Every letter really has two beginnings: the salutation and the first sentence. Both are important.

The salutation usually takes the form of, "Dear Mr. So-and-so," or "Dear Ms. Such-and-such."

It's standard practice to end the salutation of a business letter with a colon:

Dear Mr. Allen:

Dear Jim:

Dear Sir:

It is also now common business practice to use "Ms." in place of "Miss" or "Mrs." "Ms." has the double advantage of serving for both Mrs. and Miss.

However, if you're answering the letter of someone who has signed herself "Miss" or "Mrs.," use that title in your letter, as it's evidently the one the recipient prefers.

The First Sentence

In the previous paragraphs, we suggested that you begin your letter with the most important idea you plan to talk about. Now, let's refine that idea a bit.

If your letter is responding to previous communications you've had with the recipient, it's a good idea to mention it right at the beginning, before you get to your most important idea.

Here are some examples:

Dear Mr. Anderson:

As you requested in your letter of June 28, here are the prices on our grommets.

Dear Mrs. Boxer:

It was very kind of you to call last Friday and ask for information about our inn. The enclosed brochures will tell you about us.

Dear Ms. Calley:

Your Invoice No. 2345, of January 3, bills us for $24.95. We believe this is incorrect.

The reason for beginning with a reference to past communications is that it helps the person to remember exactly what he or she wrote to you about.

Complimentary Closing

The most common complimentary closings are:

Sincerely,

Sincerely yours,

Truly yours,

Very sincerely yours,

Very truly yours,

Equally acceptable, if you know the recipient, are:

Cordially,

Cordially yours,

Very cordially yours,

A few business letter writers prefer to eliminate the complimentary closing altogether. If the last sentence of the letter really ends your message clearly and pleasantly, a missing complimentary closing will probably not even be noted. For example:

> We'll look forward to hearing from you soon.
> Ralph Johansen

> Please let us know if we can help you in any other way.
> Jack Smith

─────────────── **HELPFUL HINT** ───────────────

Avoid tricky or cute complimentary closings, such as "Yours for better bargains," and "Hopefully yours." They call attention to themselves and distract from the main purpose of your letter.

SIGNATURES

Every business letter should be signed by an individual. Not only is it a courtesy to the recipient, but it also gives the recipient a human being to write to if it's necessary—a factor which is psychologically important in this computerized age. If you receive an unsigned letter from a business, you feel that nobody there cares about you; if there's a name at the bottom of the correspondence, then you feel you are in touch with someone.

Traditionally, when the writer is a man, his full name is typed below his signature:

Jack H. Jorgenson

Even if his signature uses only the first two initials, it's a good idea to type out the full name, because this gives the recipient more of a complete picture of a human being:

Women have adapted several different methods of signing and typing their names on business letters. Here are a few.

Janet Parkinson
Janet Parkinson

Janet Carter Parkinson
Janet Carter Parkinson

Mrs. William Parkinson
Mrs. William Parkinson

Mrs. Janet Carter Parkinson
Mrs. Janet Carter Parkinson

(Miss) Janet Carter
Miss Janet Carter

Miss Janet Carter
(Miss) Janet Carter

(Mrs.) Janet C. Parkinson
(Mrs.) Janet C. Parkinson

(Mrs.) William Parkinson
(Mrs.) William Parkinson

In recent years, the use of Ms. has come into wide use. Here are two ways it's commonly seen:

Ms. Janet Parkinson
Ms. Janet Parkinson

Ms. Janet Carter Parkinson
Ms. Janet Carter Parkinson

Other combinations are also possible.

———————————————— **HELPFUL HINT** ————————————————
Sign your name the way you want the recipient to address you.

POSTSCRIPTS

A postscript is a handy way to include extra thoughts which you forgot about when you were writing the letter. It's also a good way to call attention to a point which otherwise might be overlooked in the letter.

Sales letters often use a postscript as an additional enticement:

P.S. If you order before June 30, you'll also receive a beautiful leather wallet absolutely free.

P.S. If you order more than $50 worth of seeds, you can deduct 10% from the total cost of your order. It's our realistic way of saying, "Thank you."

———————————————— **HELPFUL HINT** ————————————————
A postscript will receive more attention if you write it in your own hand.

FILING NOTATIONS AT THE BOTTOM OF THE LETTER

You may find it helpful to include certain information for your files at the bottom of your letter. This information usually starts at the left-hand margin, below the signature. (See model business letters, page 20-24.)

Typist's Initials

The typist's initials tell who actually typed the letter. Sometimes they appear alone; sometimes they are preceded by the initials of the person who signed the letter.

Thus, if Elaine Carrington were typing a letter signed by Madge Ewing, Elaine might put down her own initials only, either in capital or lower-case letters:

    EC or ec

Or, she might put down both her initials and Madge's:

    ME/EC or ME/ec

Enclosures

If you're going to include something with your letter, such as a check or a brochure, you may want to indicate this at the bottom of your letter with the abbreviation:

    Enc.

Or, you may want to go into more detail:

    Enc. Brochure
    Enc. Payment Schedule

This kind of entry is useful if someone other than the typist is responsible for putting the enclosures in the envelope or if the enclosures are to be put in the envelope some time after the letter has been typed. It serves as a reminder of what's to be included.

Additional Copies

When you want copies of your letter to go to others besides the recipient, you can indicate this at the bottom of your letter in the following manner:

    Copies to: B. J. Anderson
               C. N. Carwhile
Or,
    cc: B. J. Anderson
        C. N. Carwhile

2. Good Grammar Made Painless

HOW TO SPELL CORRECTLY

IF YOU'RE A poor speller, there are several ways to improve the spelling in your business letters. First, have someone who's a good speller check your letters before they go out. Make a list of the words you commonly spell incorrectly and study them until you're sure of the correct spelling. A second way to improve your spelling is to study a good spelling book systematically. Still another suggestion is to check any questionable words against the list which follows. It combines several lists of the words most frequently misspelled by various groups and professions.

Words Commonly Misspelled

absence	benefiting	consensus	disappear
accept	buoyant	convenience	disappoint
accident	business	convenient	dividend
accidentally	busy	coolly	doesn't
accommodate		council	don't
acknowledgment	capital	counsel	during
acquaint	career	criticize	
acquaintance	catalog	criticism	
across	cemetery		effect
affect	certain		eighth
aggravate	character	deceive	embarrass
all right	chief	decide	environment
amateur	choose	decision	equipment
appearance	chosen	definite	equipped
argument	coming	descend	escape
around	commit	descendant, *or*	exaggerate
athletic	commitment	descendent	excellent
auxiliary	committed	describe	excite
	committee	description	excitement
beginning	committing	desert	exciting
believe	competition	dessert	exercise
believed	complete	develop	existence
beneficial	comptroller	difference	experiment
benefit	conscientious	different	familiar
benefited	conscious	dining	fascinate

14

February
finally
foreign
foreigners
forth
forty
four
friend

glamorous
glamour
government
grammar
grievance

hadn't
height
hero
heroes
heroine
humor
humorous

image
imaginary
imagination
imagine
immediate
immediately
individual
interest
interested
it's (contraction)
its (possessive)

judgment

knowledge
knowledgeable

laboratory
latter
literature
lonely

loose
lose
losing

maintenance
marriage
marries
marry
meant
mischievous
monetary
municipal

necessary
necessity
noticeable

occasion
occasionally
occur
occurred
occurrence
occurring
o'clock
omitted
opinion
opportunity

parallel
parliament
performance
perhaps
personal
personnel
pleasant
possess
precede
prejudice
president
principal
principle
probably
proceed

professor
promissory
promotional
pronunciation
prophecy
prophesy
purchasable

quiet
quite

receive
recommend
referred
regrettable
relieve
responsibility
restaurant
rhythm

salable, *or*
saleable

schedule
seize
sense
separate
shining
similar
simplify
society
speech
stationary
stationery
stop
stopped
stopping
strength
studied
studies
study
studying
succeed

success
successful
superintendent
supersede
surprise

technicality
tendency
than
then
their
there
they're
thousandth
to
together
too
tragedy
transferred
transient
tries
tried
truly
two

until

villain

Wednesday
weird
where
whether
woman
writ
writer
writing
written

yield
you're
your

MAKE YOUR LANGUAGE LIVELY

A business letter should be serious—but not pompous. One thing that makes many letters unbearably pompous is their use of old-fashioned or overused phrases. Here's a list of some of the more common ones. It is, necessarily, an incomplete list. The best way to screen such phrases out of your letters is to ask yourself: Is there any way I can use fewer words than I'm using now?

We acknowledge receipt of . . . Use: THANK YOU FOR
We are agreeable to your wishes . . . Use: WE AGREE WITH YOU or WE LIKE
Please advise . . . Use: PLEASE TELL
As per your letter . . . Use: AS YOU WROTE or AS YOU SUGGESTED IN YOUR LETTER
At the present time . . . Use: NOW
Attached (or Enclosed) you will find . . . Use: WE ARE ENCLOSING
At a later date . . . Use: LATER
Communication . . . Use: MESSAGE, or LETTER, or REPORT, etc.
In compliance with your request . . . Use: AS YOU REQUESTED
To date (as in "To date we have not received) . . . Use: WE HAVE NOT YET RECEIVED
Due to the fact that . . . Use: SINCE, BECAUSE
Enclosed please find . . . Use: WE ARE (I AM) ENCLOSING
For your information . . . Omit this phrase: it is usually irritating.
In order that . . . Use: SO THAT
In receipt of (as in "I am in receipt of your letter") . . . Use: THANK YOU FOR YOUR
    LETTER
In the amount of (as in "I'm sending you a check in the amount of $25") . . . Use:
    FOR ("I'm sending you a check for $25")
Prior to . . . Use: BEFORE
In the near future . . . Use: SOON
Thank you kindly . . . Use: THANK YOU
The writer (as in "The writer is happy to tell you"). . . Use: I AM HAPPY TO TELL
YOU
This will acknowledge receipt of your letter . . . Omit this phrase.
The undersigned (as in "The undersigned is happy to tell you") . . . Use: I AM
    HAPPY TO TELL YOU
We regret to inform you that . . . Use: WE ARE SORRY THAT
With a view to . . . Use: TO

SIMPLIFY YOUR PUNCTUATION

Punctuation makes it easier for the reader to understand your letter. Here are some suggestions about the most frequently used punctuation marks; they will help you punctuate easily and properly.

Period

1. Use a period at the end of a sentence.

───────────────── **HELPFUL HINT** ─────────────────
If you have any doubt about whether to use a period, use it. Then start a fresh sentence.

2. Use a period also at the end of an abbreviation such as Mr., Mrs., i.e., or viz.

Comma

1. Use commas to separate ideas in a sentence, as in the sentence you're reading right now.

2. Use commas to separate strings of adjectives. Example: We have five models: red, blue, yellow, green, and black.

3. In your letters, you'll frequently find it necessary to use commas in the following circumstances:

    a. In dates: We opened our doors for business on Thursday, March 15, 1926.

    b. In addresses: She now lives at 23 Bedford Street, Mahwah, Connecticut.

    c. When name and title are on the same line: Example:
       Richard C. Blackwell, Treasurer

    d. After complimentary closes: Sincerely,

—————————————————— **HELPFUL HINT** ——————————————————

Think of commas as short breaths in the sentence that create pauses to help increase understanding.

Colon

Use a colon:

    a. After salutations: Dear Ms. Anderson:

    b. To call the reader's attention to what is to follow: Here is a list of items we're now making: nails, screws, bolts, washers, and staples.

Question Mark

Use a question mark after a direct question: Where can I find this model?

—————————————————— **HELPFUL HINT** ——————————————————

Avoid using the question mark to express sarcasm or doubt, as in this kind of sentence: "We know you're an honest man (?)" It merely antagonizes the reader, and it is in questionable taste.

Exclamation Mark

Use the exclamation mark when you want to show special emphasis: What a sale! Never again!

—————————————————— **HELPFUL HINT** ——————————————————

As a general rule, it's better to underuse than to overuse the exclamation point. Too frequent use is like too much salt on the food: it can become distasteful.

Parentheses

The main thing to remember about parentheses is that you should be able to remove the words within them without disturbing the sentence.

This is an example of incorrect usage: "Our price (for the whole) job is $500."

This is right: "Our price (for the whole job) is $500."

3. Sales Letters That Sell

SALES LETTERS HAVE one purpose: to move recipients to do something that will eventually result in their making a purchase. You may want the recipient to place an order, to write for a catalog, to telephone, to visit your place of business, or to do any number of other things that will—sooner or later—put money in your pocket. Here are three steps that will help you compose good sales letters.

Step 1. Write down what you want to achieve. You might write: I want people to visit the store and to buy my products and services.

Step 2. List the things that will encourage the recipients to do what you want. Your list might look like this:

To get people to visit the store I can:

Offer a gift or entertainment

Emphasize that I carry the town's most complete line of hi-fi

To get them to buy my products I can offer:

A lower price on certain items

A special combination package, such as two items for the price of one

A personal warranty signed by me on anything they buy

Free consultation by factory-trained audio experts who'll recommend proper equipment for their homes

To get them to use my repair service, I can offer:

A special long-term warranty on all repairs

Discount on all repairs done in first week

Free batteries for all portable radios and TVs we repair

Step 3. Choose the most important reasons on your list and write your sales letter. Here's how it might read:

> Some very good news . . .
> There's a terrific free gift for you . . .
> And free entertainment . . .
> And great values . . .
> On Saturday, May 15.
>
> That's when the doors open at my new store—Centerville Electronics and Hi-Fi—in the Centerville Shopping Plaza.
> It will be easy to find us because the New Dixie Ramblers will be making joyful music right outside the store all day.

Just step through our welcoming doors, and you'll receive your special free gift—it's our way of saying, "Thanks for stopping in to see us."

Values? Listen to this!

You can take 40% off the retail list price on every portable radio and television in the store during our opening week.

You have a tremendous choice, because we have the town's most complete line of hi-fi equipment.

And if you buy two of our special Gold Tag items, **you'll get 50% off the retail list price.** We're glad to do it during our opening week—because we want to make as many friends as we can, as quickly as we can.

And you should know about our service department.

I've been a service specialist all of my working life, and I know we have the best repair department within a 200-mile radius of Centerville.

To back up our promise of quality, here's what we're offering:

First, a *five-year* warranty on every radio, phonograph, and television set we repair during our first week in business. As you know, most stores give three months, or at most, a year. But, because we want to meet you soon, we're giving this unusual warranty during our first week.

Second, we're giving a 10% discount on all repairs done during the first week. You'll find that our prices are always competitive and reasonable—but during this first week, you'll find they're extraordinary. We feel great about being in business, and we want to share that feeling with you.

And for good measure, if you bring us your broken portable radio or television during our first week, we'll return it to you with a set of fresh batteries, at no charge.

Come on down! We believe we have the most beautiful store of its kind in this area, and we know we offer the best values.

And I promise you: we're going to keep it that way.

Sincerely,

Marty Cogan, President

Six Things You Can Learn from This Letter

This model letter suggests some other ideas that will help you write a more effective sales letter:

1. *You* is boss. Use the word "you" frequently; it helps make the letter more like a personal conversation.

2. Use "I" contact. Notice that this letter uses the words "I" and "my." This helps to establish the feeling that one person is talking to another. The reader isn't dealing with an impersonal corporation.

3. Sign a name. A good salesperson presents a distinct personality. That's why this letter is signed with the president's name rather than with the name of the store. It's always a good idea to sign a person's name to any sales letter.

4. Break up the letter into short paragraphs: this makes it easier to read.

5. Use underlined words and heavier type occasionally: it makes the letter look more lively.

6. At the end of your letter, tell your reader what action you want them to take. In this case, there's an invitation to "Come on down!" In other situations, you might ask them to telephone or write or fill out a coupon.

MODEL LETTERS

Each of the model letters is followed by several additional suggestions which will help you to write more effective sales letters.

Arouse Curiosity

Dear Sir:

If you are open to a fresh approach to investing your money, I would like to tell you about the opportunities available in the world of Option Writing.

Option Writing is a very simple technique which many people use, with annual returns of 15% to 20% a reasonable expectation from present and growing portfolios.

If you'd like to know more about Option Writing, please call me or return the coupon below.

Sincerely,

John Christoper

Five Things You Can Learn from This Letter

Here's a simple, direct appeal to the reader's desire to make money. It uses several interesting techniques that you can adapt in your own sales letters:

1. It's short—only three sentences long.
2. It uses "you" frequently—twice in the first sentence, once in the third.
3. It's a direct letter from the writer. Although written on the letterhead of a well-known brokerage firm, it makes first-person contact with the reader by using "I," and by using the writer's signature.
4. It contains an attractive offer: the possibility of high financial returns.
5. It offers two ways of replying: through a coupon at the bottom of the letter or by telephone.

Stress Special Points

Enclosed is a $6 refund on your recent Today's People order—payable on an extra 15 months

Dear Subscriber:

(1)   This is the only time . . .

(2)   . . . that we can offer you this partial refund—to extend your new subscription more than an additional year.

(3)   Your present subscription is NOT running out, but this one-time offer won't be repeated. We urge you to take advantage of it now—while it's available.

(4)   This offer saves you more than 1/3 of today's low

(5)   rates . . . and you protect yourself against any future price increase.

(6)   It's just good common sense to insure yourself against inflation.

(7)   YOU NEED PAY NOTHING NOW. We'll bill you later because we know your credit is good. Simply let us know that you want to accept the $6 refund. It's as easy as mailing the enclosed coupon.

*   *   *   *   *

(8)   Of course, we're very happy that you're reading *Today's People* regularly. It's a sign that a thinking magazine *can* reach thinking people. We understand, it isn't for everyone—it's too difficult for most—but it's good to know that it fits your life.

That's why I hope you'll extend your subscription now.

Sincerely,

Jack Togler

Six Things You Can Learn from This Letter

1. Using a handwritten note at the top of the letter calls attention to a special point—in this case, a substantial "refund." On a letter going out to hundreds or thousands of people, the handwriting is, of course, simulated.

Other ways of achieving emphasis at the top of a letter are: printing a message with a simulated rubber stamp and using a simulated or real stamp or a seal.

2. The first sentence establishes two facts: the idea of the refund, and the fact that it's good for only a limited time. Putting a time limit on any offer introduces a sense of urgency which can help motivate the recipient to act.

3. Note that the first sentence is broken into two parts: paragraph (1), "This is the only time. . ." is followed by paragraph (2), which contains the balance of the sentence. This arrangement emphasizes the first part of the sentence and helps point up the urgency of the offer.

4. Paragraphs (3), (4), (5), and (6) explain the opening statement. *This is an important point:* They are examples of Step Two of our three-step letter-writing process: listing the reasons that will make people buy. (See page 18) Paragraph (3) stresses limited time; (4) talks about the savings; (5) discusses protection against price increases; and (6) points up the wisdom of fighting inflation.

5. Paragraph (7) makes it easy to buy. It uses the common technique of encouraging the prospect to mail back a coupon.

6. Paragraph (8) reminds them of the special value. It flatters the reader: its real purpose is to provide an additional reason for buying the product. It says, in effect: you're one of the very few, unusual people who can appreciate the finer things in life.

If the letter had started with paragraph (8), it would have gone on to talk about the many special features of the magazine and about the unique qualities of the subscribers. In other words, this letter started off talking about financial savings, and the bulk of the letter discussed that point. Another letter might have talked mainly about the quality of the magazine and its readers. The important point is that both letters would be based mainly upon their respective first paragraphs.

HELPFUL HINT

Use a variety of design effects for emphasis of words and ideas. Count the ones in the last letter—the dots at the ends and beginnings of paragraphs; the indention of paragraphs (4) and (5); the capital letters in paragraph (7); the underlined words in paragraph (8); the asterisks to set paragraph (7) off from paragraph (8).

Strong Emotional Appeal

Dear Friend:

As a youngster in New Hampshire I grew up in a home where crafts were a part of everyday life—everything from candlemaking to leatherwork, from carpentry to chair recaning.

I remember the pleasure of carving bass and bluefish lures to fish the nearby river . . . and an old friend of mine still carves sandpipers, blue herons, and fighting fish—they're works of art, really—out of wood.

A knowledge of crafts can make your life richer. And you can gain that knowledge easily with the help of the new Creative Craft Workshop. It's a series of books covering a grand variety of crafts from all over the world.

It can show you how to make beautiful and practical things at far less than it costs to buy them—clothing, furniture, decorative objects . . . things to use around the house and wonderful gifts for family, friends and associates.

Even if you've always thought of yourself as being "all thumbs," you can master these crafts. Because the Workshop will place you in the hands of some of the best craft teachers—men and women who know how to explain, as well as how to create.

If you'd like to experience the thrill of creating beautiful and useful crafts, you can do it easily.

I'll send you the Creative Craft Workshop for fifteen days—without asking for one cent in advance.

When you receive the Workshop, try out any of the projects for yourself. And if you don't like the book for any reason, return it within 15 days. And that will end the matter.

You have nothing to lose—and everything to gain.

Start now—send back the enclosed postcard, and begin to enjoy the fun that will go on for the rest of your life.

Yours sincerely,

Joseph Davidson
Editor

Three Things You Can Learn from This Letter

1. The opening paragraph is very strong: it pulls the reader right into the letter. Why? It uses the first-person technique, and it tells a story. You, the reader, are curious about what happens next. This method is a very good way to start a sales letter.

2. The letter maintains a single theme; namely, the beauty you can create with your own hands. By emphasizing this message in every paragraph, it conveys a simple, strong, consistent, and clear message.

3. The letter uses additional motivational ideas to sell the reader: look closely and you'll see that it also claims that if you buy the book you'll:

- Have a richer life.
- Save money.
- Make desirable gifts.
- Learn a skill quickly.

Bonus Offer

Dear Preferred Collector:

My letter to you today was *not* delivered by Pony Express, or stagecoach, or China Clipper. But two hundred years ago, that's probably how it would have reached you.

Mail delivery, in the early days of America, was not the common everyday event it is today. Pony express riders, skilled railroaders, adventurous clipper captains—all were involved in the great adventure that constituted the American postal system.

Very soon, all of the postal people of yesterday and today will be honored by an extraordinary new set of commemorative postage stamps.

We take great pride in bringing you the opportunity to acquire the distinguished set of Official First Day Covers of this stamp issue, *a limited, first edition.*

Please examine the enclosed brochure. It illustrates the five beautiful First Day Covers that will be available to you. Each of them is based on a different famous painting now hanging in the country's most prestigious museums.

And here is a bonus if you act now:

If you are one of the first 8,000 to reserve the set, we will include, at no additional cost, an especially distinctive Commemorative Poster.

The poster shows—in full, glowing colors—the history of the development of the American postage stamps and stamp cancellations. It is a virtual encyclopedia of stamp information, beautifully displayed on a large 2'x3' poster, printed on heavy vellumlike stock. I know it will be a keepsake that will inform, entertain, and delight you.

I urge you to use the enclosed card to make your reservation today for this unique set, which you will enjoy for the rest of your life.

Sincerely,

Preston A. Toffler
President

Four Things You Can Learn from This Letter

1. The salutation, "Dear Preferred Collector," is a variation on the more common "Dear Friend." In your own letter, think of whether you might be able to use a fresh alternative to "Dear Friend" or "Dear Sir."

2. The first three paragraphs help to arouse the reader's interest by discussing the romance of the postal service. The actual sales announcement doesn't come until the fourth paragraph. Like the previous letter, this one attempts to create a positive emotional environment for the sales message. Can your own product or service benefit from such an approach?

3. The phrase "We take great pride" suggests that this is more than a regular commercial offer, that there's something special about it. It's often possible to dress up an offer this way. Other, similar phrases include: "We invite you to be among a limited number of people who . . ."; "Once in a very great while it is possible to offer . . ."; "An unusual combination of events has made it possible to bring you . . ."

4. The poster is described in terms as glowing as those of the basic offer. The reason: while people are interested in a bonus, they'll be even more interested if the bonus really seems special. Therefore, if you're offering a bonus, dress it up in attractive terms.

4. Collection Letters That Collect

THE BASIC ELEMENT OF A GOOD COLLECTION LETTER

COLLECTION LETTERS—THOSE which you send out to persuade customers to pay you overdue sums—are also sales letters. They try to motivate the recipients to take an action which will put money in your pocket. Equally important, you want the recipients to continue doing business with you. This suggests a useful principle in writing your collection letter:

- Think about the customer in a *positive* way.
- Think about the things you can say that will make the recipient *want* to pay the debt and to continue doing business with you.

If you take this attitude, then your collection letters will tend to bring out the best in a debtor; they will make the person want to cooperate, to pay you before paying other creditors.

There is another reason for taking this approach: if your collection letters are too overtly harassing, the debtor may sue you, claiming extortion or blackmail.

TIMING OF COLLECTION LETTERS

You'll probably find it useful to have a series of collection letters, timed to go out at intervals. Each letter will have a more demanding message than the previous one. And you'll want to work out a schedule for sending the letters.

What intervals will be best for you? Only experience can give you a precise answer, but the following suggestions are standard business practice.

- Divide your customers into three groups: regular and usually prompt payers; regular but slow payers; poor payers.
- Send poor payers collection letters as soon as they become delinquent, and with the greatest frequency—say, every ten days.
- Send regular but slow payers who become delinquent collection letters at a slower rate—perhaps every twenty days.
- Send regular and usually prompt payers who become delinquent collection letters at a still slower rate—perhaps every thirty days.

The reason for this practice is that the regular and prompt payers usually don't need frequent reminders—the others do.

PERSONALIZE YOUR COLLECTION LETTERS

You will probably have a series of form letters that you regularly send out to delinquent accounts. Unless your collection notices are obviously routine forms—such as a "Past Due" rubber stamp—make your letters appear to be personalized. Address them to an individual and sign them with an individual's name. And, send them freshly typed—not printed or photocopied.

Why send a freshly typed letter? Because when the recipient sees a copy, he's likely to think that you're just going through an automatic routine. If he's intentionally delaying payment, he'll figure that it's safe to stall a bit longer.

In your business, you'll probably need to send two kinds of collection letters: form letters and personalized letters. The balance of this chapter will provide samples of both kinds.

———————————————————— **HELPFUL HINT** ————————————————————

Many businesses find it useful to enclose a postage-paid, self-addressed envelope with their collection letters. They feel it helps make it easier for the customer to pay. They refer to it in their collection letters with a phrase such as, "Just use the enclosed, postage-paid envelope for your payment." Other firms enclose an envelope but do not pay the postage. And still others don't even enclose an envelope. In your own business, perhaps the best idea is to try all three techniques to see which one works best for you.

GENERAL-PURPOSE FORM LETTERS

General-purpose form letters are those which you'll send to most delinquent customers. They may be people whom you don't know personally, and for whose delinquency you have no explanation. You may want to use all of these letters, or select only those you feel most comfortable with. Or best of all, adapt them to your own personality.

First Notice

The first notice may be simply a rubber stamp on your statement. Since you'll already have sent out one statement, this overdue notice might say:

SECOND NOTICE. PAST DUE.
THANK YOU.

If you use a different color ink for the stamp, it will stand out more clearly.

Alternative First Notice

An alternative notice could be an obviously printed form rather than a personalized letter. Print it on a sheet of paper measuring about 5 x 7 inches and attach it to your statement.

If you've already . . .

. . . sent in your payment, we'd like to thank you. But our records show that we haven't yet received it. Your business and your friendship are important to us: we want to keep them both.

If you haven't yet paid this bill, please let us hear from you by return mail.

Thanks very much,

Joe's Meat Market

Second Notice

This should be a freshly typed letter.

Dear Mr. Herman:

We want you; we need you; we count on you.

And we believe in you.

Please help us to keep our faith.

You have owed us $300 for more than two months. If it's because of an oversight, we understand: nobody's filing system is perfect. Consider this a friendly reminder, and drop your check in the mail.

If you haven't paid us for some other reason, please get in touch with us and explain the situation. I know that once we talk together, we can work out a solution that will satisfy both of us.

Sincerely,

Alternative Second Notice

Dear Mr. Herman:

Can you help me to solve a puzzle?

Your payment is now two months in arrears.

And I'm puzzled.

Have we done something wrong?

Or have you run into a problem that's causing the delay?

Please tell me about it. I'm sure we can work out an adjustment that will please you.

If the delay is simply an oversight, will you please take care of it at once.

Let's clear up the puzzle and your account at the same time.

Thanks,

Third Notice

Dear Mr. Herman:

One of the worst things about not paying bills is the feeling of failure it clamps on you—that feeling that you've failed to live up to your own expectations—and to the expectations of those who had faith in you.

If you feel that way about the $300 you've owed us for more than three months, it's understandable. But, it's also unnecessary: these problems can be solved fairly easily when the people involved talk directly and honestly together.

So, I'd like to make a proposal.

If you haven't paid because you're displeased with something we've done, will you tell us what it is? We'll try to correct it so that we can straighten out our finances.

If you've not paid us because of an oversight, please send us the amount due, and let's get rid of the problem immediately.

And, if your payment is late because you're having temporary financial problems, let us know about it. It can happen to anyone—and there's always a reasonable way to solve it.

Obviously, we want to clear up this problem. With your help, we can do it together.

Please, send us the balance due, or let us know why you're not sending it, and we'll figure out a better solution.

Alternative Third Notice

Dear Mr. Herman:

A Californian visiting Maine was boasting about the large size of West Coast lobsters.

That night, when he went to sleep, a couple of fisherman sneaked a huge 15-pound lobster into his bed.

The next morning, he awoke with a howl and jumped out of bed, the lobster clamped firmly to his big toe.

"My God! What is that thing?" cried the Californian.

"Oh, that?" shrugged one of the Maine men. "That's just a Maine bedbug."

Mr. Herman, the $300 you have owed us for the past three months may seem to you like a tiny bedbug of a debt; but it's a monstrously big sum to us.

We want to continue doing business with you. But, this debt makes it virtually impossible to continue. So, we'd like to make a couple of suggestions.

First, pay us the entire amount within the week, and we'll be able to grant you the kind of credit we've done in the past.

If that isn't possible, call me or drop me a line explaining the problem, and we'll work out another solution.

Sincerely,

Fourth Notice

Dear Mr. Herman:

Please, tell me.

Have we come to the end of our business relationship?

And must we now go through the expensive and unpleasant mess of litigation?

If you will pay the $300 you've owed us for the last four months, we can continue doing business together. (Personally, it's the course I'd prefer, because I believe we can be helpful to each other in the future.)

If you can't pay the full amount, please get in touch with me by the end of the week. If we can work out a satisfactory arrangement, we can still do business together.

But, if I hear nothing more from you, then I'll have to turn your account over to my attorney.

What shall I do? You tell me.

Sincerely,

Alternative Fourth Notice

Dear Mr. Herman:

We know you are honorable.

We, too, are honorable.

As honorable men, it's important to be honest with each other in all our dealings.

The facts are these.

You have not answered the three letters we've sent you, asking for payment or for a statement of when we may expect payment.

If we hear from you within five days, we will withhold your file from our attorneys.

Otherwise, we shall have no alternative but to turn your account over to them for collection.

I know that as an honorable man and as a businessman, you will want to avoid the expense and publicity of going to court over an unpaid bill.

Sincerely,

Naturally, once you say that you plan on turning the matter over to your attorneys, the next collection letter should come from a lawyer. If you send another letter saying, in effect, "I'll give you one more chance," you've undercut the force of your threat, and your letter will probably be ignored.

INDIVIDUAL COLLECTION LETTERS

An individual collection letter addressed specifically to the person who owes you money may be more effective than a form letter. The trick is to make it appeal to the specific situation of the debtor. Here are some basic things to think about before writing a personal collection letter:

1. Can you guess why you haven't been paid? Is the customer temporarily short of funds? Or is he traditionally a very slow payer, or is he having personal problems—illness, for example—that may be the cause of the delay?

   If you know the cause of the delay, think about whether your letter will be stronger if you refer to the cause directly.

2. Does the customer have any special interests that might help motivate payment? For example, if he's a passionate golfer, you might refer to his sportsmanship, or if he's devoutly religious, you might appeal to his sense of ethics.

3. Do you know the customer socially? If so, you should be especially careful in the wording of your letter. Remember that after the debt is settled—or even if it never is settled—you'll probably still be seeing him. Consider whether your letter will make it more painful for you in your subsequent social life, and indeed, whether or not you care about it.

SAMPLE PERSONAL COLLECTION LETTERS

Letter Sent to a Customer Offering Discount Incentive

Notice three points about the following letter. First, it's a personal letter from the writer to the recipient. That personal "I– You" feeling runs throughout the letter.

Second, it's a sales letter as well as a collection letter. That is, it offers a persuasive reason for paying the debt: a special discount.

Third, it concludes with a definite date by which payment is expected. This helps the recipient: instead of leaving him with a vague thought that he can put off paying for a few weeks, it sets up a specific deadline for him to meet.

> Dear Mr. Anderson:
>
> I want to tell you how personally sorry I am to hear of the difficulties you've been experiencing in your business. I'm sure that your years of experience and your natural acumen will soon have you back in full swing.
>
> Naturally, I want to help you out in any way we can, since you've been a good customer for many years.
>
> We think we can extend some help on your credit account with us. As you know, it is now $500, and it is two months late. I assume that the delay is related to your current difficulties.
>
> Here's how we can help you. Normally, you pay within 30 days and take a 7% discount.
>
> Naturally, the discount is forfeited after 30 days. But, as a gesture of goodwill, I'm creating a special discount of 4% on your account. I'm enclosing a new invoice showing the new discount. I know you're anxious to maintain a good credit relationship with us—and so I'll look forward to receiving your payment by January 23.
>
> Best wishes,

Letter Sent to a Customer Who's Traditionally a Slow Payer

The following letter uses several techniques which you may be able to adapt:

1. It starts out on a positive note: the writer speaks directly about the fact that he enjoys doing business with the customer.
2. It praises a characteristic of the customer's: he's an individualist. Such a customer probably prides himself on going his own way, on not following the crowd. This letter congratulates the recipient for the trait.

   This approach helps the customer to feel more secure, more self-confident, more responsible, and more responsive.
3. The letter does not accuse the customer of delaying payment. Instead, it calls the customer's attention to the fact of a late payment. In other words, instead of saying, "You're a bad person because you haven't paid," it says, "You're a good person, and I want to call your attention to a situation which you'll want to correct."
4. The letter warns that the "special relationship" may change if payment is not forthcoming. But it does this in a positive way by stating that the payment will permit a continuance of past business relations.

Dear Mr. Jansen:

I enjoy doing business with you because you're an independent thinker—a man who follows his business instincts, regardless of how the crowd runs. It's a rare virtue, and I admire it.

Naturally, over the years, I've learned to adjust to your patterns, and I feel it's been worthwhile.

But I have to alert you to a bad situation which needs your immediate attention.

As you know, most customers pay in full after 30 days. In the past, you've enjoyed a special relationship and have paid in 60 days.

Now your bill of $150 is 100 days past due.

If the delay is an oversight, I know you'll want to take care of it immediately. If you're dissatisfied for some reason, let me know, and we may be able to make an adjustment.

I respect your independent judgment because it's fair. I ask you now to exercise your sense of fairness and to pay the full balance by the end of the week—June 14.

I look forward to your payment so that we can continue doing business together in the future as we have in the past.

Sincerely,

5. Answering Collection Letters

THE ART OF answering collection letters calls for as much skill as the art of writing collection letters. If you receive a collection letter, there are a number of alternatives open to you:

1. Send nothing, and hope for the best.
2. Send nothing, but send a letter explaining why you're sending nothing.
3. Send all or part of the amount due, with or without a letter of explanation.

This chapter will discuss ways of responding to a collection letter when you're sending only part of the amount due—or none of it.

SOME BASIC GUIDELINES

1. If you can't pay what you owe, and if your main goal is to gain time, then your letter should be designed to reassure the creditor that his or her money is safe because you're honest and you plan to pay it back as soon as possible. *Giving reassurance* is the major goal of writing responses to most collection letters.
2. Lay down a plan for repayment. This is the best way to reassure your debtor that you deserve the time you need to make the payment. If possible, state how much you plan to pay back each time period; that is, how much you plan to pay back each month, each quarter, or whatever.
3. Mention your personal wish to clear up the matter. Your creditor wants to know that you're taking the debt seriously: reassure him or her about it.
4. It's often useful to explain honestly why you're unable to pay fully what you owe. This helps to establish more human contact between you and the creditor.

PARTIAL PAYMENT

The following letter is a good model for a covering letter to be sent with partial payment of a debt. Note how it's organized.

The first paragraph states that the money is enclosed.

The second paragraph apologizes for the delay and explains why it happened.

The third paragraph states what the writer plans to do in the future.

The fourth paragraph expresses the writer's sincerity.

The final paragraph expresses appreciation.

Your own letter need not follow this outline exactly, but it should touch all these bases.

Dear Mr. Jorgenson:

I'm enclosing $50, a partial payment of my debt.

I'm sorry that I fell behind in my payments. A sudden family illness has drained off much of our income, and it has taken us a while to readjust.

I think we are on top of the problem now, and I plan to resume regular monthly payments to you.

You understand, I'm sure, that I take this debt seriously, and that I do want to pay it back as quickly as possible.

You've been most patient, and I appreciate it.

Sincerely,

John Klinger

REQUEST FOR PAYMENT DELAY

When you have to ask your creditor for an extension, use the following letter as a model. Note the organization:

The first paragraph sets the mood: it asks for understanding. (This paragraph can be eliminated if you feel uncomfortable with it: it's essentially a matter of personal taste.)

The second and third paragraphs explain the reasons why a payment delay is being requested.

The fourth paragraph makes the specific request—and tells when payments will be resumed.

And the last paragraph promises a return to normal payments.

Dear Mo. Framor:

This is a difficult letter to write because it imposes on your goodwill. But I am relying on your understanding to help us through a difficult period.

A series of events has made it necessary for us to miss our regular payment schedule.

Among those events was the unexpected death of our accountant at a time when he was analyzing our books. It will take us a while to get them back in order. In addition, we have had an unusually large number of delayed accounts receivable, and as you can imagine, this has delayed our payments. However, we are now taking steps to reduce those accounts to normal proportions, and we expect to be back on an even keel within a very short time.

Therefore, I'm asking that you grant us a delay of 60 days in our payments. We will plan to start our regular payments on or about June 15.

After that time, we expect to return to the regular business arrangement we have enjoyed with you for many years.

Sincerely,

Bonnie Mart Gifts

EXPLANATION AFTER A LONG SILENCE

When you've let a creditor go for a long time without an explanation, a letter may help to soothe angry feelings. Here's a model that you can adapt to your own situation. Note the paragraph organization:

The first paragraph offers an apology.

The second and third paragraphs explain why payments have been late.

The fourth paragraph explains what the repayment plan will be.

And the last paragraph ends on a personal note, expressing appreciation and looking to the future.

Dear Mr. Trenton:

I'd like to apologize for this overdue explanation of our late payments.

The fire which destroyed our warehouse last month triggered several other problems. Only now that we're getting them under control have I had a chance to sit down and answer your letters requesting payment.

As you know, during the past year we had a number of problems which left us with a severe cash shortage. Among the most severe of those problems was the dissolution of our company partnership. This required us to pay a large sum of cash, leaving us in a rather tight cash squeeze. This was one of the major reasons for the relative slowness of our payments during the past year.

Now, however, all that is behind us. We have set up plans to repay our creditors. We plan to start by the first of next month, and you can look for a partial payment at that time. Thereafter, we plan to send you payments regularly, covering not only current billings but the past-due amounts as well.

In this way, within the year, we expect to be on a completely current basis with you.

I'd like to thank you for your patience throughout this trying period. And I look forward to many more years of good business relations.

Sincerely,

B. W. Marks Company

NON-PAYMENT BECAUSE OF BILLING ERROR

When you receive an incorrect bill, the simplest procedure is to write a letter explaining why you're not paying it and giving the relevant details.

Note the organization of the following letter.

The first paragraph states the problem: the bill is in error.

The second paragraph explains in detail why there's an error.

And the third paragraph offers to give further information if necessary.

Dear Mr. Warder:

Your notice of January 12 says that we owe you $15.00. I believe your records are in error.

On December 15, we paid you $275 with our check No. 372A. That sum covered several items, including the $15 in question.

If you have any questions, please write or call me, and I'll be happy to discuss the situation. Otherwise, I'll consider the matter straightened out to your satisfaction.

Sincerely,

G. & M. Dry Goods

NON-PAYMENT BECAUSE OF DEFECTS

You may not have paid an invoice because the shipment was defective in some way. Your letter of explanation should explain clearly why you're withholding payment and what you expect the creditor to do about it. Use the following letter as a general model. Your own situation, of course, may differ substantially, and it is a good idea to obtain legal advice if you have any doubts.

Dear Mr. Greene:

On July 20, we received a third and "final" collection notice for $27.95.

As I mentioned in my letter of March 12, we believe that we should not pay this sum, since the merchandise for which you're charging us was so defective as to be worthless.

If you wish, you may send your representative to pick up the unused portion of the material. Our Mr. Antrim will be glad to return it.

We respectfully suggest that you adjust your billing records accordingly.

If you'd like to discuss the situation, please call me or Mr. Antrim.

Sincerely,

The Curiosity Shop

ASKING HELP FROM THE CREDITOR

If your own financial affairs have become so hopelessly entangled that you despair of solving them, it may be useful to call upon your creditor for help. At the worst, the creditor may refuse; but it's more likely that he or she will see it as an opportunity to collect at least a part of what's owed, and you may be able to get considerable help. Use the following letter as a model.

The first paragraph asks for help.

The second paragraph states the problem briefly.

The third paragraph holds out hope of payment.

The fourth paragraph asks for specific aid in setting up a new payment schedule.

And the last paragraph reassures the creditor of the debtor's intent to get back to a regular payment schedule.

Dear Mr. Alberts:

I'd like to ask your help in straightening out my financial problems with your company.

As you know, I am quite overdue in my payments.

However, I believe that over a period of time, it will be possible to pay off the entire debt. And I should very much like to do that.

Therefore, I'd like to work with you to set up a revised payment schedule. What information would you like to have in order to work out a realistic schedule?

You may be certain that I plan to cooperate with you to the best of my ability in order to clear up this situation and bring our relationship back to normal.

Sincerely,

Bruce Frost

6. Writing Letters of Inquiry

LETTERS OF INQUIRY are those which seek information. We can divide them into two kinds: simple and complex.

A simple letter of inquiry asks for information which probably already exists: for example, it may request a catalog, or specification sheets, or product literature, or price lists.

A complex letter of inquiry asks for information which may not exist in the form you want it and which will have to be put together in order to get you an answer. These letters usually require some thought if you're going to get the information you want.

HELPFUL HINT

Use any reference numbers that may be helpful. For example, if you're inquiring about an insurance policy, list the policy number, if you know it; if you're asking about a part for a piece of machinery, give the model and serial number of the machine; if you're discussing a credit card matter, give your credit card number.

SIMPLE INQUIRY LETTERS

For a simple request, all you need is a simple letter.

> Gentlemen:
>   Please send me your latest catalog and price list.
>
>   Sincerely,

When trying to find out what a supplier has that might be useful to you, give as many details as the recipient will need to send you what you want.

In the following letter, for example, the writer tells what the material will be used for, i.e., winter suits. This permits the recipient to make a relevant selection.

> Gentlemen:
>   Please send me sample swatches of wool fabric suitable for men's winter suits.
>   I'm interested in all weights and colors.
>
>   Yours,

COMPLEX INQUIRY LETTER

The fundamental rule for writing complex inquiry letters is: make them easy for the reader to understand. As a general rule, include the following kinds of information:

1. Explain why you're making the inquiry.
2. Give a detailed list of all the separate pieces of information you want. Unless you're specific about your needs, the recipient is likely to take the path of least resistance and give you less, rather than more, information.

In the following letter, the first five paragraphs provide facts that will help the recipient to answer intelligently. The balance of the letter describes the specific information that the writer is requesting.

Gentlemen:

My company is planning to hold a national sales meeting in your city around the first week of April.

We will have about twenty people at the meeting.

They will probably arrive the night before the meeting begins and stay for two additional nights.

We will need two conference rooms throughout most of the time, each capable of holding about 10 people.

We would also like to arrange special entertainment for them in the evenings.

Please let me know:
1. The rate scales for single- and double-occupancy rooms.
2. The cost for meetings rooms.
3. The details of any package plans that offer room, meals, and some form of entertainment.
4. What kind of attractions you can offer the spouses during the meeting sessions.

If you need additional information in order to answer my questions, please call or write me.

Sincerely,

"SELLING" AN INQUIRY

An inquiry may also be a sales letter—especially if you're trying to encourage the recipient to give you a serious answer. The inquiry which follows is an example of this kind of message. After you read the letter, look at the analysis which follows it.

Gentlemen:

We are planning to expand our present business—the selling of epoxy coatings for industrial and commercial floors.

We are looking for additional, related products which our sales force can offer.

Our firm is one of the oldest of its type in this area. Our reputation is excellent, and our credit rating is quite high. We're planning this expansion in order to serve better the needs of our customers, who are coming to rely on us more and more for maintenance supplies.

Our sales force operates primarily in New England.
The products and services we can represent competently include:
Floor maintenance and cleaning items
Mats, carpeting, and other floor coverings
Drain tiles and sub-flooring specialties
Floor maintenance contracts
Window-cleaning contracts
If you'd like to explore the possibility of having our company represent you, I'd be happy to have you write or telephone me. If our aims mesh, I believe it can be mutually profitable.

Sincerely,

Analysis

The first paragraph explains who the writer is and what the writer wants to accomplish for his firm.

The third sentence describes the company's reputation: it's a way of encouraging the reader to pay serious attention to the letter.

The remainder of the letter gives additional information that the writer thinks will help the reader answer intelligently.

Notice the last paragraph: it ends optimistically, mentioning the possibility of profit. It's not a hard-sell ending, but it does leave the reader with the feeling that this is something worth looking into.

QUESTIONNAIRES

The questionnaire is a special form of inquiry which you may find useful in your business. With a questionnaire, you're writing the same letter to many people, and you'll usually be asking several questions.

For example, you may be surveying customers to find out if they're satisfied with your service, or if they're aware of your advertising campaign, or if there are other services or products you can offer them. The reasons are virtually endless.

In most cases, you probably won't be offering the people anything for answering your survey, so you've got to make it very easy for them to participate. Here are some suggestions which will be helpful:

1. *Keep it short.* Ideally, make it less than a page in length. (The major exception is when the recipients are as interested in knowing the results of the survey as you are: for example, if you're taking a survey of the members of a club or a school and you plan on publicizing the results. As a case in point, every year, *Consumer Reports* magazine distributes a survey to subscribers. The survey usually runs at least four pages, but they get a large response because the subscribers know they will benefit by getting better information about things they intend to buy.)

2. *Keep it simple.* Probably the best questions are those that can be answered by a "Yes" or "No." Multiple-choice answers should permit the reader to check one out of three or four answers, such as: "Like it very much . . . Like it a little . . . No strong opinion . . . Dislike it."

3. *Give a good reason for responding.* When requesting answers to the questionnaire, explain how the results will benefit the reader. For example, if you're a retail store surveying customers, you may be able to promise a better selection of merchandise or more accommodating store hours. If you're a manufacturer, you may be able to

promise a better quality product or a line of items more nearly attuned to the customer's needs.

4. *Enclose postage.* Enclosing a self-addressed, stamped envelope will usually increase the number of responses you'll receive.

─────────────── **HELPFUL HINT** ───────────────

The hardest part of any questionnaire is deciding on the questions to ask. You'll often find that the question which first comes to your mind doesn't elicit an answer which will be very helpful. So, it's important to define for yourself precisely what you want to know. Once you've written your questions, try them out on a couple of friends to make sure that their answers will give you the kind of information you want.

Retailer Questionnaire

Dear Customer:

Morse's is your store. And we want it to be the kind of place you really enjoy visiting—even if it's just to browse. So, we're very interested in getting your opinion about how we can make ourselves more to your liking.

If you'll check off the answers to the few questions below, it will help us to make our store the kind of place you want it to be.

Thanks ever so much,

Jim Patton, Manager

1. Did you have to wait too long for a salesperson?
Yes _____ No _____
2. Did you feel the salesperson was helpful to you?
Yes _____ No _____
3. Was the salesperson's knowledge of the merchandise:
Excellent _____ Fair _____ Poor _____
4. Was the quality of the merchandise:
Very good _____ Fair _____ Poor _____
5. Did you feel the merchandise was priced:
Too high _____ About right _____
6. How often do you visit this shopping center? _____
About once a week _____ About once every two weeks _____
7. About how often do you visit our store?
About once a week _____ About once every two weeks _____
Less than once every two weeks _____

The Questionnaire as Sales Tool

A questionnaire can also be used as a sales tool. Here, for example, is one which inquires into the customer's feelings about the services rendered by a rug-cleaning company. At the same time, it lets the customer know that the company offers other services as well.

> Dear Customer:
>
> Are you satisfied with the work we've done for you? Is there some way we can do a better job?
>
> Will you take about two minutes to check your answers to the questions below? They'll help us keep our service at a high level.
>
> And if you'd like to make any other comments, simply use the back side of this sheet.
>
> If you'll tuck the questionnaire into the stamped, self-addressed envelope and send it back to us, we'll be very grateful.
>
> Sincerely,
>
> Mrs. Marjorie Harrington
> President

1. Did our pick-up people come at about the time we said they would?
   Yes ☐ No ☐
2. Were they polite? Yes ☐ No ☐
3. If they had to move furniture to roll up the carpeting, were they:
   Very careful ☐ Not too careful ☐ Careless ☐
4. Were your carpets and rugs returned when we said they would be?
   Yes ☐ No ☐
5. Were they cleaned to your satisfaction? Yes ☐ No ☐
6. If you asked us to make repairs, were they done satisfactorily?
   Yes ☐ No ☐
7. Do you know that we offer the following cleaning services:

	I knew it	I did not know it
Furs	☐	☐
Drapes	☐	☐
Leather apparel	☐	☐
Regular laundry services	☐	☐
Hand-laundering for fine items	☐	☐

8. May we use your name as a reference? Yes ☐ No ☐

If you'd like to make any special comments, you can use the reverse side of this sheet.

Thank you again for selecting us to clean your rugs and for answering this questionnaire.

7. How to Answer Inquiries

IT'S WORTH GIVING considerable thought to the way you answer inquiry letters. Because, if your letter is unclear or cold, or if your answer shows that you haven't read the inquiry clearly, it will make you look silly, incompetent, unfeeling—or all three.

On the other hand, a well-written answer to an inquiry can win respect. And equally important, it may turn the inquirer into a customer—or at least, a booster.

Here are the principles to follow in answering letters of inquiry:

1. *Answer the question.* Usually this is no problem, because most inquiries are simple and direct. But, some of them aren't—and these are the ones that can embarrass you if you answer them incorrectly. So, read the letter carefully to make sure that you answer the question that's been asked.

2. *Be friendly.* Even when you have to turn down a request or answer that you can't really give the information wanted, be nice about it. (Further on in this chapter, you'll find a couple of examples of this type of letter.) The rule is: smile when you have to say no.

3. *Be brief.* This, of course, is a general, all-purpose rule: regardless of what kind of letter you're writing, it should be as brief as it can be.

4. *Be prompt.* To delay is to irritate. Why irritate when, with a little care, you can delight the inquirer with your promptness? Some companies have a policy: every inquiry has to be answered within 24 hours after it's received—even if the reply simply says that a more detailed answer will come later.

5. *Follow up.* On some inquiries a follow-up letter may increase the chances of making a sale. Maintain a separate file of these letters so that you can send these people follow-up letters. On pages 46 and 47 are some examples.

FRIENDLY REPLIES

A pleasant letter in answer to a request for a catalog or for literature can create a friendly atmosphere conducive to buying. Here are two examples: the first one emphasizes a kind of homey friendliness; the second has a more businesslike quality. Either letter can be typed individually or sent as a form letter.

Homelike Friendliness

Dear Mrs. Johnson:

I'm delighted to send you the catalog you requested.

All of us here are very proud of this year's items—it's the most attractive group we've had in a long time. And as you probably know, we've been famous for many years for the remarkable quality of our products.

This year, though, it's really something special. I know you'll enjoy the catalog. And even better, I know you'll enjoy turning your dreams into reality by ordering.

I'll look forward to hearing from you.

Sincerely,

Businesslike Friendliness

Dear Mr. Anderson:

You'll find this year's catalog offers you an amazingly wide and attractive assortment of styles.

As you leaf through, you'll see that we've kept the wide selection of popular items for which we're famous. And we're especially proud of our new line of imported items, which begin on page 30. They provide very high quality at a very moderate price. It'll pay you to study them closely.

I'll look forward to serving you.

Sincerely,

─────────────── **HELPFUL HINT** ───────────────
Take a tip from mail-order experts and use the pronoun "I" instead of "we." Even in a form letter, "I" creates a feeling that the writer is talking directly to the reader. "We," on the other hand, usually creates a sense of distance and anonymity. In business correspondence—as in most human affairs—the writer who takes personal responsibility has an advantage over the one who tries to pass in the crowd.

POINT TO SPECIFIC INFORMATION

Some inquiries can be answered by literature which covers a great deal more than the inquirer asked about. In those cases, a good reply will tell the reader where to look.

Call Attention to Certain Pages

Dear Mrs. Jenkins:

Your letter of June 13 asks for suggestions on matching and contrasting colors for a child's bedroom.

You'll find some terrific ideas in the new booklet I'm sending you, which shows all of our latest paint colors.

Look especially at pages 34 through 37, which describe some marvelously attractive bedrooms. I'm sure you'll find at least a dozen ideas that will brighten your walls. They also, incidentally, show some perfectly brilliant window treatments.

If you'll look in the Yellow Pages of your telephone book under "Paint Stores," you'll find several in your area that feature our colors. I know they'll be glad to help you in any way that they can.

And so will I—if I can be of any further assistance.

Cordially,

Janet Harper
Color Coordinator

The letter only answers the inquiry by referring to certain pages in the catalog; it also goes on to make it easier for the reader to find the product, by suggesting that she check in the Yellow Pages. This is a simple idea which can be applied to a wide variety of nationally distributed products.

As an alternative, the letter might have given the name and address of a specific store or representative in the prospective customer's area. Here, in fact, is a letter which does exactly that:

Recommend a Salesperson

Dear Mr. Sawyer:

You recently wrote to ask us about our security systems—about costs, maintenance contracts, and related matters.

To give you an overall picture of how our equipment works, I'm sending along some literature that has just come from the printer. So, it's very up-to-date.

However, pricing is a highly individual matter, since every installation is unique. As you'll see from the literature, we agree with the police and other experts that no one security system will satisfy everyone's needs. A good system is one which is adapted to you: you shouldn't have to compromise your needs in order to fit what we design.

So, I've asked our representative in your area, Ms. Margaret Wesson, to telephone you. She'll be able to answer your questions, so that you can decide for yourself which kind of system is best for you. You'll be hearing from her within the next week or so.

Sincerely,

DELAYED RESPONSE

Some letters require responses from several different people, because no one person has all the information. You might send an immediate response which (1) lets the person know that you've received the inquiry and are working on an answer, (2) tells the person how soon an answer can be expected. This second point will eliminate the recipient's worry about whether you've forgotten him in the interim.

Dear Mr. Anderson:

It will take us a couple of weeks to answer fully your letter asking us about the formulas and manufacturing processes of Royale Polyethylene.

I'm dropping you this note to let you know that we *are* working on a complete reply, and we'll be in touch with you as soon as we've put it all together. You should expect a response in about two or three weeks.

Sincerely,

WHEN YOU HAVE TO SAY NO

Among the more difficult letters to respond to are those which make a request to which you have to say, "No." They can range from the relatively simple "no," when you don't handle a product or a service, to the complicated "no," which may involve some delicate or ticklish reasoning.

It's worthwhile, when you write a rejection letter, to keep in mind how the recipient is going to feel: the likelihood is that he'll feel some sense of disappointment. If you care about this—and it's good business practice as well as good human relations to care—then you'll think about how to be helpful. That extra bit of thoughtfulness pays off in the long run: people like to do business with people who care.

Here's a variety of examples and analyses.

A Simple No

When you receive an inquiry about a matter which has nothing to do with your company or your department, respond in a way which is clear and, if possible, helpful. One way of being helpful is to suggest other places that might be more helpful.

> Dear Mr. Matthews:
> I wish we could give you the information you've asked for about plastic sheeting. However, we're not in that business.
> You might be able to find the information by checking for manufacturers in the Yellow Pages of your telephone book. Or, your library's Reference Department might be able to give you some leads.
> I'm sending along a brochure which describes the products we do make. If you have any questions about these, I'll be glad to try to answer them.
> Good luck in your search.
>
> Sincerely,

HELPFUL HINT

When you have to respond that you can't answer an inquiry for information, think about whether you can suggest the standard sources of reference information: the Yellow Pages; the local public library; and business, trade, and professional associations.

Rejection of a Request

When you have to turn down a request that you might be able to accept at some other time, be especially considerate.

One way of being considerate is to phrase your response in positive rather than negative language. For example, the following letter might have begun:

> Dear Mr. Conway:
> We're sorry that we have no space available . . .

This kind of beginning is clear and straightforward enough, but it also creates a negative impression because it begins with a negative idea: "We're sorry . . ." Contrast this with the beginning in the letter which follows:

> Dear Mr. Conway:
> We'd like very much to have had you with us during the Christmas season, but because our room reservations were very heavy this year, we had to stop accepting reservations about a month ago.
> If you can visit us at another time, we'd be happy to see you. It's usually wise to make Easter reservations about two months in advance.

We do hope that you'll think about visiting us soon. The beach has never looked lovelier, and we're getting a variety of new and colorful birds nesting in the area.

Sincerely,

───────────────── **HELPFUL HINT** ─────────────────
Try to get as many "good" thoughts as possible in a letter of refusal. In the letter above, note that every paragraph begins with an invitation to try again. This leaves the recipient with the feeling that the writer really cares about him.

Rejection for Competitive Reasons

You may have to write a letter rejecting a request for information which your company doesn't want to release. A courteous explanation is a convenient way to respond:

Dear Ms. Normand:
Your assignment sounds fascinating, and I suspect it will lead you to some interesting discoveries.
We'd like to answer your questions about the formulation of Minarex, but we have to keep this information confidential for competitive reasons.
However, I'm sending along an article from a recent industry magazine which will give you a good overview of our company and our competitors.
Good luck in your research project, and if I can help you in any other way, I'll be happy to try.

Sincerely,

Note that the above letter refuses to give requested information, without once saying "no." Note, also, that the writer sends along other information which may or may not be useful—but which indicates a cooperative, friendly attitude.

FOLLOW-UP LETTERS

After your first response to an inquiry, you may want to send a second letter to encourage the recipient to take some action.

A good follow-up letter reminds the recipient of the original inquiry and response; repeats or summarizes the information in the first letter; and may offer additional incentives for the recipient to act.

Dear Ms. Wallace:
A few weeks ago I sent you a price list for our yarns. In another month, we plan to have our annual spring sale, and I wanted you to know that you can now save about 30% off on that list.
I'm sending you our sales announcement now, so that you can place your order in advance and take advantage of these lower prices.
As you probably know, we have the largest assortment of yarn in this section of the country, and we're famous for the personal attention we give each order.
Will you let us serve you soon? I'd love to have a chance to add you to our family of good friends and customers.

Sincerely,

Sometimes you can use a follow-up letter to encourage a sale after a first sale has already been made.

Dear Mr. Jodrell:

We wanted to tell you some good news.

You'll recall that a few months ago you ordered letterhead stationery and envelopes from us. We hope that you were pleased with them. And we think you'll be equally pleased with a new product.

We've recently begun to offer our customers an exciting new idea: business cards with your photograph on them, in full color, at a very reasonable price.

As you'll see from the enclosed brochure, they're very attractive. Perhaps even more important, they are practical: they remind your customers of you much more vividly than a traditional card. That's why so many large and progressive companies now issue them as a standard practice.

We're offering the new cards at a special, introductory price, described in the enclosed brochure.

I know you'll be pleased with them—I now use them myself, and I'm getting terrific response. I'm sure you will, too.

Sincerely,

8. Complaint Letters
That Get Action

THERE IS AN art to writing good complaint letters. The art is in knowing how to stay calm. In perhaps 80 percent of the situations calling for complaint letters, a calm approach will get you further than anger. As for the other 20 percent, anger can be helpful if you know how to use it to motivate the recipient to do something—rather than simply using it as a means of venting your wrath.

So, let's ask the question: what's the best way to write a complaint letter? The answer is: before you write a word of your letter—in fact, before deciding what you want to say—decide exactly what you want to achieve:

Do you simply want to express indignation?

Or do you want a refund?

Or do you want the recipient to be more careful next time?

Or do you want to tell the recipient that you can no longer do business together?

Or do you want a credit?

Whatever you want to achieve, get that one fact fixed clearly in your mind. *In fact, it's often helpful if you write it down on a piece of paper. That one sentence may become the beginning or the end of the final draft of your letter.*

You might write down:

I want a refund.

I want them to exercise better quality control.

I want them to know that if this happens again, I'll switch to another supplier.

Now, put that paper aside, and think about whom you want to write to. If you're writing to someone who already knows about the situation and is likely to remember it immediately, you'll write one kind of letter. If you're writing to someone who won't be familiar with the situation immediately, you'll write a different letter, because you'll first have to explain the problem.

In deciding whom to write to, the critical question may be: who's the person who's most likely to be able to help me? Is it someone I'm used to dealing with? Or is it somebody higher up—perhaps the president of the company? If you're not sure, it may be a good idea to think about writing to the president.

Why? The president may be too busy to read your letter but will most likely see that it's passed along to the right person. And the chances are that it will be sent with a note attached to it—perhaps an innocuous note which says, "Please take care of this."

The person who receives a note from the president is likely to pay close attention to it—and this increases the likelihood that you'll get fast action.

An anecdote will illustrate the point. I bought a car-top luggage rack which fell apart the first time I used it. I wrote three complaint letters: one to the president of the store where I had bought the carrier, suggesting that he drop the model from his line because it was unsafe. A second went to the president of the company that made the carrier, requesting a refund. And the third went to the president of the conglomerate company which owned the firm that had made the rack. In that letter, I requested the president to look into the matter because the subsidiary company's products were hurting his entire conglomerate's reputation.

In short, each president received a letter asking him to take a different action.

Within a week, I received a telephone call from the president of the luggage rack company offering not only to send a refund but also to give me a more expensive model free. He also complained that it was unnecessary for me to have written the other two; they had both called him and told him to take corrective action, and he wasn't happy about that kind of pressure.

That kind of pressure, of course, is exactly what's often necessary in order to get action in business. And, since it may be a lot faster and less expensive than working through lawyers, it's well worth a try.

After you've decided what you want to achieve with your letter and who you're going to write to, here's a simple step-by-step procedure to follow that will help you to get your letter written quickly, clearly, and forcefully.

First, at the top of a fresh sheet of paper, write down what you previously decided you wanted to achieve. You might write: "I want a credit," "I want them to exercise better quality control," or "I want them to know that if this happens again, I'll switch to another supplier."

Now, imagine that you are saying these words directly to the person you're writing to, and change them accordingly. For example, you might change, "I want a credit," to "I want a credit of $75 because you made a mistake for that amount in your billing."

Or, you might change, "I want them to exercise better quality control," to "I want you to exercise better quality control over the castings you sell me."

Or, you might change, "I want them to know that if this happens again, I'll switch to another supplier," to "I plan to switch to another trucking firm unless you can provide better service."

Next, imagine that the person you're talking to knows nothing about the situation, and that you're explaining it for the first time.

In the case of the first example, you might write:

> I want a credit of $75 because you made a mistake for that amount in your billing.
> If you'll check your invoices, you'll see that I've ordered a total of $75 worth of merchandise since my last payment. But you've billed me for twice that—$150.

Now, add a final sentence saying what you want the recipient to do, or what you plan to do.

> Please send me a new statement for the correct amount of $75.

Let's take the next example. Notice that the last sentence describes what action the writer is going to take.

> I want you to exercise quality control over the castings you sell me. I have had to discard about 10% of every shipment for the past year.

I have spoken about this to Jane Dale, your sales representative, at least three times. She has always promised to get it corrected. But nothing has changed.

I like your prices and your delivery schedules, but I'm throwing away too much of your merchandise.

If you can't cut down on the percentage of poor castings, I'm going to start deducting 10% from your statements.

Now let's look at our third example.

I plan to switch to another trucking firm unless you can provide better service.

During the past six months, your driver has arrived at our loading docks from half an hour to an hour late.

Every time this happened, we suffered major delays with our other shippers, and our schedules had to be completely realigned.

If we have similar problems next month, we will not renew our contract with you the month after that.

I hope you will do whatever needs to be done to make sure that your driver arrives at the right time from now on.

Now, you're ready for your final editing.

The first letter might be stronger if we eliminate the first half of the first sentence. So, the final letter might look like this:

Dear Mr. Jansen:

Your company made a mistake in its billing.

If you'll check your invoices, you'll see that I've odered $75 worth of merchandise since my last payment. You've billed me for twice that—$150.

Please send me a new statement for the correct amount of $75.

Sincerely,

As we reread the second letter, it seems that the first sentence has become less important than the second sentence—and that the letter might be improved if we dropped the first sentence. The final letter might look like this:

Dear Harry:

For the past year, I've had to discard about 10% of every shipment we've received from you because of poor quality workmanship.

I've spoken about this to Jane Dale, your sales representative, several times. She has always promised to get it corrected.

But nothing—absolutely nothing—has changed.

I like your prices and your delivery schedules. But I have to throw away too much of your merchandise.

And I can't afford this kind of waste.

Therefore, from now on, I plan to start taking a 10% discount on your bills unless you can eliminate the bad castings.

Sincerely,

Finally, let's look at our third example. Here, the first sentence is a strong one; it will get the attention of anyone who reads it. And since we want attention paid to the letter, we'll keep it. The letter seems to require no major changes, so we'll send it off as is.

Let's review those steps, because they'll serve as a guide in writing almost any complaint letter:

1. Write down what you want to achieve.
2. Decide whom you're writing to.
3. Use the statement you wrote down as the first statement of your letter.
4. Modify that statement so that you're saying it directly to the person you're writing to.
5. Give any additional explanatory facts that will enable the recipient to understand why you're writing.
6. Tell the recipient what action you plan to take or what you want him or her to do.
7. Examine the letter to see if you can improve it by eliminations, changes, or additions.
8. Send it off.

Here are some other suggestions you'll find helpful.

1. Ask yourself if it will be helpful to send documentation of your complaints. Do you have invoices or other records to substantiate your statements? And if so, will it help if you let the recipient see them? If it will, make copies and include them. **Note: Never send the originals; you risk losing them.**

Also, if you send several documents, identify each one clearly. You can mark them "A," "B," "C," etc., at the top in large letters, and refer to them that way in your letter. This will make it easy for the reader to refer to them.

Dear Mr. Manson:

I'm distressed to learn that you've apparently lost our shipment. To help you locate it, I'm enclosing a copy of the trucker's shipping receipt (marked "A") and an itemized list of the contents (marked "B").

Document "C" is an insurance form which you should fill out if you cannot find the shipment.

Sincerely,

2. If you're writing to someone who's directly and fully responsible for your problem, you may be safe in saying, "You did such and such," or "You're responsible for such and such." But usually, it's better to phrase it, "Your company did such and such," or "Your people are responsible for . . ."

This puts the recipient in a position where he can take some action without having to defend himself.

See the difference: first, an example of a complaint blaming the recipient.

Dear Mr. Handleman:

You've made a mistake in our order no. 12345. We asked for blue, and you sent us green. This is the third time you've made an error like this, and if you can't prevent it from happening, we'll have to stop doing business with you.

Sincerely,

Now, let's see the same letter with the complaint directed at the company:

> Dear Mr. Handleman:
>   Your people have made a mistake with our order no. 12345. We asked for blue, and they sent us green. This is the third time they've made an error like this. If they can't prevent it from happening, we'll have to stop doing business with your company.

3. In complaint letters, it's especially important to be as specific as possible about names, dates, times, amounts of money or merchandise, etc. They help make your letter more realistic, and more businesslike.

ANGRY LETTERS

As suggested before, use anger sparingly. It's very hard to give the full sense of your anger on paper—the reader is isolated by time, by distance, and by paper.

If you are going to be angry, think about your choices. You can be angry just at the beginning of the letter, or toward the end, or throughout. Whatever you choose, it's a good idea to put the letter aside for a few hours and then reread it. You may find that you want to make major revisions: anger has a way of distorting what you really want to say.

You can be angry at just the beginning of the letter. In this example, after the initial attack, the letter calmly reviews the facts.

> Dear Jack:
>   You've put me in a very difficult position, and I'm quite unhappy about it. I hope this letter will be a step toward correcting a situation which I can no longer tolerate.
>   Let me review what's happened.
>   Two months ago you agreed to supply me with a filmstrip promoting the new product we're introducing.
>   Since we were working under a tight time limitation, I promised to give you my corrections within 24 hours after receiving them from you. As you know, I've lived up to my part of the bargain.
>   Now, we're two weeks past deadline, and there is still about another two weeks of work to be done.
>   I feel that you should put extra people on the job in order to complete it by January 15. If you're unable or unwilling to do this, please let me know immediately, and I'll arrange to have someone else take over the job.
>
>   Sincerely,

Or, you can be angry at the end of the letter. The following letter calmly reviews the facts, then ends with righteous anger.

Dear Mr. Fredericks:

I want to call your attention to the poor work that your crew did on our company landscaping project.

Here are some of the things I've noticed:

We contracted for 50 conifers; I can find no more than 30.

We contracted for a low hedge along the driveway. There is none.

We contracted for drainage tiles to prevent puddles on the driveway after rain. The driveway is a virtual swamp after the rain.

I can point out at least ten other deficiencies—and I plan to—when you visit us for a personal look at this work.

Frankly, I'm outraged at what I consider to be an amateurish level of workmanship and the carelessness of your crew. I'm not sure which is worse—the poor supervision or the poor craftsmanship—but together, they've combined to really do us in.

Please call me and we'll set up a date for you to see for yourself—and to take corrective action.

Sincerely,

9. Answering Complaints Effectively

YOU'VE GOOFED. YOU'VE made some kind of mistake— perhaps you billed a customer incorrectly. Perhaps the customer is unhappy about the service you gave.

Or, perhaps you haven't goofed at all: but the customer is complaining anyway because he or she thinks you've made a mistake.

How can you best answer the complaint?

The first thing is to decide what you want to achieve in your answer. Do you want to apologize? Do you want to make amends? If the customer has demanded more than you're willing to give, do you want to negotiate? Or do you want to tell the customer that he or she is wrong; that as far as you're concerned, the complaint is unjustified?

Once you've made up your mind about what you want to achieve with your letter, you'll be in a much better position to write it.

A GENERAL FORMULA

Here's a formula that may be helpful when you write your own letter.

First, thank the writer for sending you the letter, and express regret that the person had cause to complain.

Second, tell what you plan to do about it.

Third, give an explanation, if one is necessary, and tell why the situation will not recur.

Fourth, thank the recipient again for letting you know about the problem.

Here's how the formula works out in a basic model for a letter:

Dear Mr. Smith:
   Thank you for your letter of (DATE).
   I'm very sorry that you had a problem with (DESCRIBE THE PROBLEM VERY BRIEFLY).
   We're going to (DESCRIBE WHAT YOU'RE GOING TO DO TO RESPOND TO THE COMPLAINT).
   The reason that the problem arose is that (GIVE A BRIEF BUT PLAUSIBLE EXPLANATION).
   The problem should not occur again because (TELL WHY, BRIEFLY).
   Again, thank you for writing us and for giving us a chance to correct the matter.

                                        Sincerely,

This model, of course, will not cover every situation, but it does provide a basic framework which you can adapt in answering many of the complaint letters you receive. Now, let's look at some specific real-life situations.

CORRECTING A COMPLAINT

Dear Mr. Roberts:

We're very grateful that you let us know about our billing error of $75.50.

We're correcting it at once, and are sending along a credit memo for the same amount.

Thank you for telling us about the problem so quickly. We're glad we're able to clear it up immediately.

Sincerely,

REJECTING A COMPLAINT

Naturally, some complaints are unjustified. When you respond to one of these, it's a good idea to (a) express appreciation for the letter; (b) politely explain why the complaint is unjustified; and (c) finish up with another expression of thanks.

Dear Mrs. Folger:

We appreciate your letting us know that you feel we've billed you incorrectly. Naturally, we want to correct any error that we've made.

You say that we neglected to credit your account for $5.75 in returned merchandise. We believe we've found the source of the problem.

Your August bill was $28.28. You paid that in September, and requested a credit of $5.75 for a blouse which you had returned.

We credited your account for that amount in our September bill.

If you'll re-examine your September bill, you'll see the credit entered as the last item.

This, of course, is why the credit doesn't appear in the October invoice.

Again, we do appreciate your writing. If you have any questions, I hope that you'll write or telephone me.

Sincerely,

─────────────── **HELPFUL HINT** ───────────────

When answering a letter in which the writer makes an unjustifiable complaint, avoid such expressions as, "You're wrong," or "You've made a mistake." They simply antagonize the reader, since no one likes to be told that he or she is in error.

Instead, use such phrases as, "The facts, as we understand them, are . . ." or "As we see it . . ."

NEGOTIATING AN ADJUSTMENT

When a customer demands a greater adjustment than you're willing to offer, consider making a counter offer. The following letter provides a good example of that.

The letter also illustrates another point: even when you disagree with the customer, you can say that he's right. Note how strongly the first paragraph is worded to create the feeling that the writer of this letter is completely on the side of the person he's writing to.

An alternative—but inferior—beginning would be: "Dear Mr. Rollison: I'm afraid that I can't agree with you completely . . ."

> Dear Mr. Rollison:
>
> You're absolutely right: our fertilizing and hedge-trimming service should have been better. And you do deserve an adjustment on your bill.
>
> You suggest that we cancel it altogether.
>
> I think this would be reasonable if our service representative had done nothing of value for you. However, he did mow and aerate your lawn.
>
> The regular fee for mowing and aeration is $25.00. I suggest that we invoice you not for the full $25.00, but for $20.00. In that way, you won't be billed for service which was below standard, and as a sort of rap on the knuckles for us, we'll swallow part of the mowing bill.
>
> On the assumption that you'll agree to this arrangement, I'm enclosing a new invoice for $20.00.
>
> Naturally, I'm personally concerned about the matter—and I've taken steps to see that it won't happen again.
>
> The man who did the job on your lawn had a hard session with me. In the future, I think you'll find that he'll do the kind of first-rate work we had come to expect from him.
>
> If you have any further problems, please call me at the office any weekday. You know that we value your business, and we want to do everything in our power to make you happy with our performance.
>
> Sincerely,

COMPLAINTS YOU CAN'T REMEDY

When you receive a letter with a justifiable complaint about something you can't change, how should you handle it? The letter which follows provides considerable help.

The letter is a response from the president of a waste-disposal firm to a citizen who had written an angry letter complaining about noisy drivers, noisy trucks, and early collection hours.

Read the president's response, and then read the analysis directly below it.

> Dear Mr. Holloway:
>
> (1)   Your points are well taken, and I have to agree with virtually all of them.
>
> (2)   Our refuse trucks do make noise; they do wake up some people in the early morning; and our drivers do talk louder than is sometimes necessary, especially at that hour of the morning.
>
> (3)   We can immediately do something about the drivers. I've had a meeting with them and asked them to lower their voices, and I know they will.
>
> (4)   In explanation, it may be helpful to remember that to hear each other over the sound of the engines, they have to talk loudly. So, when the engines aren't running, they sometimes continue at the same volume. I believe that since I've spoken to them, you won't be bothered by it.

(5)   I wish that we could solve the noise problem and the early-hour collections as easily.

(6)   Today's refuse trucks operate with very powerful hydraulic crushers, driven by strong and—unfortunately—noisy engines.

(7)   We are always looking for newer and more effective equipment, and when quieter machines become available, I assure you that we will consider buying them.

(8)   As for the early collection hours, we are pretty much locked into them by the requirements of our customers, and of the general public, which objects strongly if refuse is allowed to lie around on the streets once the day gets under way.

(9)   It may help to know that 20 years ago, before we had developed present technology, we used to have to start an hour earlier in the mornings. So, some things are improving.

(10)   I've written you this detailed answer because I know that you're concerned about these problems, and I want to assure you that I am, too.

(11)   We are trying to provide our community with the best possible service, and we need the understanding of people like you. I hope this letter will help to explain the nature of our work and how we're trying to contribute to a better environment.

Sincerely,

Analysis

In paragraphs (1) and (2) the writer immediately agrees with the justice of the complaints. This makes the recipient relax and feel more receptive to the explanation that follows.

Paragraph (3) describes what action has been taken as a result of the complaint. This, again, helps create a good feeling on the part of the complainer. It's always satisfying to know that you've had some effect on another person.

Paragraph (4) gives an explanation of the problem. The paragraph isn't necessary, but it does create a "context" for the complaint; it explains that it was a natural, human incident.

In paragraph (5) there's a positive response to a complaint. It avoids negativism by agreeing that the problems need to be solved.

The opposite approach would be to say something like, "I'm afraid we can't help you on the noise . . ." or, "We can't do our job properly unless we collect in the early hours." This negativism causes, at the very least, a feeling of disappointment in the reader's mind. Why do this when it's so easy to make the reader feel right instead?

Paragraph (6) explains why the problem exists.

Paragraph (7) is important because it says: "We are interested in solving this difficult problem; we're on your side, and as soon as we can do something about it, we will." The opposite approach would be: "Don't blame us, blame the machines. It's not our fault." This, of course, is most unsatisfactory to the recipient, because it says, "I don't care about your problem."

Paragraphs (8) and (9) serve the same function as paragraph (6). They explain why the problem of early collections exists.

Paragraph (10) shows the personal concern of the writer.

Paragraph (11) expands the idea of concern and ties the issues to the community's welfare. This helps to put the entire letter on a higher plane; it says, in effect: "We are all in this world together, and I, as a businessman, am doing my best to make it a better world.''

JUSTIFIED COMPLAINT ABOUT SALESPERSON

When you have to answer a complaint about rudeness, the easiest way may be to accept the blame, tell how you plan to prevent its recurrence and apologize.

Dear Mrs. Jacoby:

Thank you for telling me about the salesman who waited on you last Thursday.

I've discussed the matter with him, and he has assured me that it will not happen again and that he is very sorry the incident occurred.

I believe that part of the difficulty was that we were all extremely harried that day. It was the opening of our post-Christmas sale—and in the rush, he simply got carried away.

As for myself, I'm quite sorry that the incident occurred, and I apologize for it.

We do value your friendship, and we hope that you'll come back very soon and give us the opportunity to show you that courtesy is our first order of business.

Sincerely,

JUSTIFIED COMPLAINT ABOUT A PRODUCT

One way to answer a justified complaint about a defective product is to send a new one.

Dear Mr. Hartnett:

First, we're sending you a pound of fresh nuts to replace the stale ones you bought. I believe you'll find them every bit as delicious as our ads claim.

Second, I want to tell you how sorry I am that the package you bought was less than perfect.

We do try to ensure freshness by making sure that our stores return merchandise after a certain period. Apparently, there was an oversight, and your package overstayed its welcome.

I want to thank you for calling it to my attention; I'm dropping a note to the store, asking them to be more careful.

In the meantime, I hope you enjoy the contents of the new package. We're especially proud of the crop we're currently packing, and we think you'll notice the difference.

Sincerely,

REJECTING AN UNJUSTIFIED COMPLAINT

Sometimes you just have to say, "No." Usually, it's when someone sends you a complaint that you feel is utterly unjustified.

One good way to answer is to explain nicely why you feel it's unjustified, and then, if possible, make some other offer. This may be particularly useful if the writer of the complaint is a customer whom you'd like to keep.

The following letter is an example of this kind of response.

Dear Mrs. Carter:

I certainly sympathize with your concern: you think that you overpaid us for your car because your friend bought the same model for $200 less.

There are several possible reasons for the difference.

First, the two cars may have had different accessories and options; naturally, this would cause a price difference.

Second, your friend may have offered a trade-in.

Third, your friend may have bought the car from a dealer in a different area, where overhead costs are lower than ours. Naturally, in such a case, the cost of the car may be lower.

Fourth, your friend may have bought the car during a special sale.

There are other reasons for price differences—but those I've listed tend to be the main ones.

Perhaps that will explain why we're unable to grant you the $200 refund you request. The price you paid was the standard price for the car with the options you selected.

But we will make this offer: we'll put you on a special mailing list that keeps some of our customers informed of especially good buys that come into the shop from time to time.

We know it will be another year before you're ready to buy a new car, but we do want you to be aware of all the opportunities available. In this way you can be prepared when you're ready to buy.

In the meantime, we know you're going to enjoy your purchase. It's undoubtedly the best-made, best-looking model the company has ever produced. And you can be confident that you made a very sound investment.

Sincerely,

10. How to Write Good Memos

MEMOS ARE REALLY business letters in disguise, and in writing them, you should follow the same principles that you use in writing good, basic business letters. If there's any major difference between a memo and a letter, it's that the memo may be shorter and written in a terser style.

We can divide memos into two broad groups: short, informal ones and longer, more formal ones. The short ones may consist simply of one or two sentences, and they may be handwritten. The longer ones may run from a paragraph on up to several pages, and they are usually typed.

HELPFUL HINT

If you write a lot of short memos, consider whether it will be worthwhile to buy commercial note pads. Office-supply stores have a variety of printed forms. Some are pads of single sheets; some contain single, double, or triple carbon copies. You can get them in a variety of colors and sizes, and if you want, you can have your name or company letterhead printed on them. Your local printshop can make up custom-tailored memo pads for you at a reasonable price.

BASIC MEMO FORMAT

Whether it is a long memo or a short one, it is a wise idea to include the following information:

The date

Your name

The name of the recipient

Names of people who are to receive copies

Longer memos also often have a one- or two-line headline summary at the beginning.

Here's a standard format for a memo:

January 14
To: Janet Flanner
From: Bill Conway
Subject: Status of Engineering
1. All the drawings requested are enclosed, with two exceptions:
  a. Number 456—Smokestacks
  b. Number 32-A—Rudder

2. Both are being redrawn and will be sent to you by next week.
3. Please return everything when you're finished.

cc: Mary Halpern
    Ted Lapidus

The preceding memo uses a number in front of each major point and letters in front of minor points. It's not necessary to use numbers and letters, but it does help to ensure that the reader won't skip anything important. It also helps you, the writer, make certain that there's a reason for each point you put in the memo.

The abbreviation at the bottom of the memo, "cc," means "Copies are being sent to":

SHORT MEMO REQUESTING ACTION

12/14
Joe:
Please send this Parcel Post. Thanks.

                                        Harry

This informal note has all the basic information necessary for a good memo. It has the date, the name of the recipient, and the name of the sender. It's usually a good idea to date memos in case a question arises later about when they were sent or received. Short as the memo is, notice that it's polite, including both "Please" and "Thanks."

PRINCIPLES FOR WRITING LONGER MEMOS

There are only two basic principles to think about in organizing your ideas for a longer memo.

The first basic principle of memo writing is: decide the main purpose of the memo. Is it simply to give the recipient a résumé of what happened at a meeting? Or is one or more of the recipients going to have to take some action as a result of your memo? In either case, your memo should make this purpose clear.

If you have trouble writing memos, you may find it helpful to jot down the purpose before you start. You might write something like this:

Purpose: to tell my boss what decisions we made, just to keep her up to date.

Or, you might write something like this:

To tell committee members what happened at our subcommittee meeting, so they can take appropriate action.

Or, you might write:

To recapitulate main decisions reached at the meeting so everyone present will remember what we agreed on.

The second principle of good memo writing is: stick to the essentials. It may help to ask yourself, "What are the three most important things to cover?"

Write them down on paper before you write your memo. If you can get a clear statement about the most important points, you'll usually find it easier to know what you want to say. (Three is an arbitrary number; there's nothing sacred about it. But often, if you put down more than three, it becomes difficult to focus on the most important ones; and with fewer than three, you may be leaving out important material.)

For example, if you were reporting to your boss about a committee meeting for the office Christmas party, you might jot down this outline:

1. Agreed to have the party Dec. 23.
2. Posters and invitations to be finished by Dec. 1.
3. Office Party Fund to finance it: $75 estimated cost.

Now, let's see how these principles can be applied to writing good memos.

INFORMATION MEMO

Let's assume that you've written down that the purpose of the memo is to tell your boss what decisions your Christmas party committee made. And, let's assume that the three most important things that happened in your meeting are the ones listed in the previous paragraph.

Your memo might look like this:

Nov. 20
To: Roseanne Vogel
From: Chris Harwell
Subject: Christmas Party Committee Decision
The Christmas Party Committee met Nov. 19 and made the following decisions:

1. This year's Christmas party will be held Dec. 23.
2. We'll have posters and invitations finished by Dec. 1.
3. We'll request $75 from the Office Party Fund for expenses.

Everything is progressing nicely, and there are no problems. Next meeting will be Dec. 5.

MEMO REQUIRING SIMPLE DECISION

Suppose that you wanted to report the same information as in the previous memo, but in addition, you needed your boss to make a decision.

You can modify your "Subject" line at the top of the page to call the boss's attention to the need for the decision:

Nov. 20
To: Roseanne Vogel
From: Chris Harwell
Subject: Request for Decision on the Christmas Party
The Christmas Party Committee met Nov. 19 and decided to:

1. Hold the party Dec. 23.
2. Have posters and invitations finished by 12/1.
3. Request $75 from the Office Party Fund for expenses.

Decision to be made: Where shall we hold the party? The committee was divided evenly between holding it in the office and holding it at a restaurant. If you have a strong feeling one way or the other, please tell me, and that will be it.

MEMO REQUIRING A DIFFICULT DECISION

When you send a memo asking someone to make a difficult decision based on information in the memo, it's helpful if you neatly lay out the factors on which the decision is to be based. Here's an example:

April 17
To: J. C. Grew
From: R. T. Polk
Subject: Request for Decision About Ad Campaign Launch Date

1. The purpose of this memo is to have you decide on a date for launching our Product X ad campaign.
2. Some of us feel the launch date should be July 4. Others feel we should wait until after Labor Day. Here's a summary of the arguments.
3. Those who favor July 4 say:
   a. It will tie in nicely with the national holiday.
   b. It will be a popular summer item.
   c. We can start a second campaign after Labor Day.
   d. Our salespeople can focus on Product X because our other products move slowly in summer.
4. Those who favor waiting until after Labor Day say:
   a. Summer is always our slow period and Product X would be hurt if launched in summer.
   b. A second post-Labor Day campaign would be too expensive and anticlimactic.
   c. Our sales reps have enough to do selling existing products in the summer; selling Product X puts an unnecessary burden on them.
Personally, I favor waiting until after Labor Day, mainly because of the burden it will impose on the salespeople before then.
   I'd appreciate a decision by May 1.

                                                        Thanks

Notice that the preceding memo gives the writer's opinion. This may be useful if the recipient places any special value on the writer's thoughts. If, however, the recipient doesn't, then the opinion may be out of place.

MEMO MAKING AN INQUIRY

If you're asking for information, it's a good idea to give a deadline:

To: Harry Magnuson
    Jerry Fury
    Jack Wallace
From: Tom Slade

I'm making up year-end reports for our division, and I need the following information about your department:
   1. Present number of employees
   2. Number at beginning of year
   3. Total present staff payroll, including exempts and nonexempts.
Please have this information to me by Dec. 3. Thanks.

If the deadline were very important, you might want to emphasize it by putting it first:

> *Urgent deadline: December 3!*
> By Dec. 3, I must have the following information from your department for our divisional year-end reports:
>   1. Present number of employees
>   2. Number at beginning of year
>   3. Total present staff payroll, including exempts and nonexempts.

MEMO FROM MANAGEMENT

Among the most difficult memos to write well are those that management sends out to lower-level employees. They tend to be stiff, stuffy, formal, and off-putting. Why does this happen? Frequently it's because the boss feels awkward about having to issue written orders—and the awkwardness and stiffness leak into the memo.

What can be done to prevent this? One way is to develop the right attitude. If you're the boss and you're writing to a group of lower-level people, picture yourself writing to *just one* of them rather than to several. Select the one you like the most or have the most respect for, and imagine that you're writing exclusively to that person.

Second, consider using some form other than the traditional memo format, which frequently looks stiff when it's meant for group distribution.

Let's see how a typical, stuffy memo from the boss can be transformed into a message which will make people want to cooperate.

Stuffy Version

June 12
To: All Employees, Accounting Dept.
From: J. B. Totten, Department Manager
Subject: Leaving the Office Early

1. It has come to my attention that a number of Accounting Dept. personnel have been leaving for the day between fifteen (15) and twenty (20) minutes early.
2. This practice cannot be allowed to continue.
3. All Accounting Dept. staff are expected to stay on the job for the full working day. Anything less than that will be considered cause for penalty.

Unstuffy Version

PLEASE BE FAIR

Please stay on your job until quitting time—5:00 P.M.

Leaving early is unfair to the rest of the people, who are putting in a full day's work.

If you have a special reason for quitting early, tell your supervisor, and he or she will okay it. Otherwise, we'll have to lay down stricter rules.

Thanks for cooperating,

Jack B. Totten

What are some of the differences between the two memos?

Tone. The first one is stiff and authoritarian. The second is more conversational, as if one person were talking to another.

The first one says: "Do as I say or I'll hurt you." The second one says, "Let's work together." The second one is better because it appeals to people's better instincts and makes them want to do the right thing.

Heading. The standard "To/From/Subject" heading is clear enough. But since this is a memo that will either be posted on a bulletin board or distributed to each employee, a stronger beginning, like the second memo's "Please Be Fair," will understandably get more attention.

First paragraph. While the first paragraph of the first memo is clear and straightforward, it sounds pompous. This is probably because it's a public memo: if it were addressed to one person, it might seem less stuffy. Also, it's redundant to write the numbers as digits after writing them as words, as in "fifteen (15)."

The first paragraph of the second memo immediately states the purpose. It gets to the heart of the matter more quickly.

Second paragraph. Again, notice the difference in tone. The first memo is almost strident. The second talks about the fairness to other employees. Again, the second memo asks the employees to think about doing right, while the first tells them to be afraid.

Third paragraph. The first memo finally delivers its message: stay on the job for the full day or you'll be penalized. The second memo suggests that if there's a special reason for going, you can arrange it—but cooperation is necessary to avoid stricter rules. And notice that the second memo ends with another positive note: "Thanks for cooperating."

Signature. The second memo gives the manager's first name: this is more friendly than the initials given in the first memo. Further, the second memo does not give the manager's title. If everyone in the department knows him, there's no point: giving the title merely emphasizes his importance, which doesn't need emphasizing. On the other hand, if the department is so large that everyone doesn't know his name, then it will be useful to put in the title.

─────────────── **HELPFUL HINT** ───────────────
To make long memos clearer, it's often a good idea to use brief, explanatory headlines at the beginning of each new group of ideas. For example, if you begin with a general explanation of what's behind the memo, your headline might be, "Background" or "Introduction." Other frequently used headlines include: "First Main Point," "Second Main Point . . ."; "A Look at the Future"; "Where Do We Go From Here?"; "Recommendations"; "Summary"; "Conclusion."

11. Business Communications That Build Goodwill

YOUR BUSINESS PROBABLY needs all the goodwill it can get—and you can get a surprisingly large amount by telling people about yourself through the mail.

For example, many companies send out newsletters to tell customers about new developments of interest.

Others send follow-up letters one or two months after a customer's last purchase.

Still others send out bulletins to special customers announcing special sales.

And many send special Christmas or other holiday greetings.

In this chapter we'll discuss all of these kinds of letters—and some others.

NEWSLETTERS

At their best, company newsletters are a way of making the recipients feel that they're getting useful and interesting news—news that will help them to do a better job or become better informed. Basically, there are two kinds of company newsletters: those meant primarily for use within the company and those meant primarily for external use (that is, for customers and prospects). Some companies make one newsletter serve both purposes.

In the following paragraphs, we'll focus on the external newsletter.

A good first step is to think about what you'd like the newsletter to do for you. For example, if you're a distributor or wholesaler, you might use it to alert customers to special seasonal deals. If you're a retailer, you might use your newsletter to tell about special sales and to offer public service information. If you sell a service, such as a bowling alley or a lawn care business, you may want to tell about new contracts or additional services you're offering.

Chances are that you'll think of at least two or three things you'd like the newsletter to accomplish for you. Write these down, and put them where you'll be reminded of them whenever you're putting your newsletter together. They'll guide you in your selection of material.

Next, you'll want to think about frequency of publication. How often will it be practical for you to put out the newsletter? Once a month? Bimonthly? Once a quarter? Twice a year? Or, at irregular intervals? After you decide what you can reasonably accomplish, stick to the schedule: people will come to rely on it, and its effectiveness will gradually increase.

Another decision to make is: who'll write it? Do you have the time and the ability? Or, will you delegate the job? Take this responsibility seriously once you decide to go ahead with it—the only way to ensure publication is to be certain that whoever does it has the time and the talent to put the newsletter together.

You'll also want to select a name and a logotype for your newsletter. The logotype is a design for the title of your newsletter, and it usually appears at the top of the first page. You may pick up a design you're already using—on your business card, for example—or you may have an artist draw one for you. Or, the logo may simply consist of the name of your newsletter in a distinctive type.

Contents

As you put together the items for your newsletter, refer to the list you made of the things you want the newsletter to accomplish for you. Each item that goes in should be related clearly to that purpose.

For example, if you're a hardware dealer and you've decided that the main purpose of your newsletter will be to promote seasonal merchandise, most of the information in the newsletter should tie in to the season. If it's a Christmas promotion, you'll feature items that sell well at Christmas. And if you include other items, such as home-care tips, they should be relevant to Christmas. For example, information on how to string Christmas tree lights would be a natural.

If you decide to include news about new sales personnel, this too can be slanted toward the season. As a case in point, the caption under a photograph of a new salesperson might say, "Dan Jenkins, our newest salesman, is an expert in the small hand-tools that make such perfect gifts for your home handyman. Dan was born and raised in Boston, and he now lives in Weymouth with his wife, Jenny, and his two sons, Tommy and Fred. Dan's also a life-long angler, and he'll be happy to answer any questions about suitable presents for the fisherfolk on your Christmas gift list."

Layout

The appearance of your newsletter is important, because it will create a strong impression of the kind of company you run. It will simplify your job if you settle on a basic layout and stick to it issue after issue. That is, select the number of columns on the page, the kind of type you'll use for the text and the headlines, and the color of the ink and paper. One way to do this is to discuss it with someone with experience. It may be a local printer, or an artist, or a designer. He or she can set up the basic format, which you can follow in succeeding issues.

Study the Others

Get to know what other companies are doing with their newsletters. For a couple of weeks, collect all those that come to you in the mail, and ask your friends and associates to do the same. Look them over, compare them, and see what you like and don't like. Then, you'll be much better prepared to put together your own, very effective newsletter: a steady, useful builder of goodwill.

SALES FOLLOW-UP LETTERS

Sales follow-up letters remind customers that you feel they're important and that you're seeking their business. They provide an excellent opportunity to develop new orders from your best prospects, that is, from those who have already done business with you.

RETAIL STORE SALES FOLLOW-UP

A general-purpose letter to all customers who haven't made a purchase for a while should do more than invite them back. It should give *reasons* for them to come back—a new line of merchandise, a new service, or a special sale. Here's an example of a letter that a retail store might send to customers:

Dear Mr. Anton:

It's been a couple of months since you've used your charge account with us, and that probably means you haven't been in to see our latest additions: several new ideas in office supplies designed to reduce your operating expenses.

Among the most exciting items:

● An electronic stamping machine that will stamp and seal packages in half the time and for 10% lower cost than traditional machines;

● A digital read-out scale that can save you 5% of every dollar you spend for postage;

● And a new line of ballpoint pens that cost less than pencils.

We have a lot more that's new and different, which you'll enjoy seeing.

I'd be very pleased to show you these items and to discuss any other needs that you may have in office supplies. Please come by soon, so we can renew our acquaintance and show you some of these new expense-cutting ideas.

BUSINESS SERVICES FOLLOW-UP

A useful way to follow up on a customer is to provide him or her with new, useful information. In the case of a business service, it may be a new provision of the law that the customer should know about. Here's an example of such a letter. It was sent by an accounting firm at the end of the year—when prospective clients were beginning to think about hiring accountants to handle their income tax returns.

Dear Ms. Derthik:

You may be able to take advantage of some new provisions of the Internal Revenue Service. These provisions can reduce your taxable income this year by letting you put a greater amount in your individual retirement plan.

I'm enclosing an article that explains this in some detail, along with the forms that need to be filled out if you elect to take advantage of the new provisions.

And of course, if you have any specific questions, I'll be very happy to answer them. You can call me any weekday.

Sincerely,

INVENTORY CLEARANCE

A way to build goodwill with regular customers is through special sales. Here's a letter from a manufacturer to his regular customers. The semihumorous tone is right for this kind of junk sale.

Dear Mr. Ferris:

My partner Bill and I are having a whale of an argument and you can help settle it. It's about garbage.

At least, Bill says it's garbage and we should throw it out. I say it isn't—and that it's worth something to someone.

We have a tremendous supply of miscellaneous items we've been accumulating for nearly a decade. Some of it is raw materials we bought too much of: things like ten-foot steel, aluminum, and brass rods; 200-foot-long coils of heavy-duty electric wiring; perhaps 50 pounds of assorted ball and roller bearings; and at least a couple of thousand yards of blue denim.

Some of the stuff is finished or semifinished pieces that we've turned out over the past year: metal lawn furniture, fireplace sets, baby carriages, and the like.

Some of it is in perfectly terrible shape. And some of it is in first-rate condition. We can't use any of it—but for the person who can, it's a terrific bargain.

Everything is marked at crazy prices—a 1,000-foot role of heavy twine for a buck, five-gallon metal buckets for 75¢ each, two-drawer filing cabinets for 5 bucks a throw.

We're putting it all on sale for our regular customers the week of April 14. The week of April 21, we'll offer what's left to the general public.

And the week after that, it all goes to the dump.

So come and get it. Even if you don't need it, how can you afford to turn down a bargain like this? If you like, bring the kids and let them carry the stuff for you.

We'll look forward to seeing you then.

Sincerely,

A NEW SERVICE

One way of building goodwill for a salesperson is for the boss to write customers in advance to let them know that the salesperson will be calling or visiting with useful new information. This can be especially useful with a prospect or a past customer whom the salesperson is not currently calling on. (For a variation, see Letters of Introduction in the next chapter.)

Dear Joe:

In a few days, you'll be getting a call from Dan Merton, a new salesman who's going to tell you about an ingenious delivery service we're planning, which will save you money and eliminate a lot of aggravation.

The service is different from anything now available: it's tailored precisely to your needs—and we can usually pick up your shipments within 45 minutes of the time you're ready to ship.

Dan will tell you about it—I simply wanted to let you know that you're going to discover a better way of doing business than you ever could have imagined.

Cordially,

HOLIDAY CORRESPONDENCE

It's standard practice, of course, for businesses to send out holiday greetings at Christmas. Usually, it's in the form of a card, but a letter might be a welcome change—especially for good customers.

Dear Anna:

This year, I want to send Holiday wishes in my own words rather than with a card.

Over the years, you've been a good, steady friend; and although our relationship has been basically related to business, I've often felt that business was merely an excuse for something more important: a mutual respect and sincere liking for one another as human beings.

At this time of the year, when we all think of Peace on Earth, I wanted to say a few words directly to you, wishing you a very Merry Christmas and a Happy New Year.

Sincerely,

MORE HOLIDAY CORRESPONDENCE

There's no reason why holiday greetings have to be confined to the Christmas Holiday greetings have to be confined to the Christmas Holiday. In fact, an argument could be made that it's better to send greetings at some other time of the year, when the customer is less swamped with mail.

Dear Mr. Jainworthy:

With the approach of Independence Day, everyone's getting ready for fireworks, nostalgia, and more than the necessary quota of speeches expressing appreciation for our way of life.

It's also, of course, about half way through the year. And it seemed to me that this is a good time to let you know that we're very appreciative of the business you've given us over the years.

I suppose everyone has his own interpretation of what constitutes "the American way." I think you have to include honesty, integrity, and a willingness to work with the other person. Those qualities certainly characterize the way you've dealt with us over the years, and I wanted simply to say, we appreciate it, and we hope to be able to serve you in the future as we have in the past.

Sincerely,

ANNIVERSARY LETTER

Dear Floyd:

Do you remember what happened on the afternoon of October 15, five years ago?

According to my appointment book, that was the day I first called on you to see if I could interest you in taking on a new line of men's and boys' clothing.

I remember still the impression you made on me: you were extremely courteous, even though you let me know that you weren't going to buy from me that season. But you also gave me the feeling that I should keep trying.

I'm glad I did. It's meant a lot of good business, and more important, it's meant getting to know a very fine person.

We usually don't get a chance to say these things because we're so busy meeting deadlines, but I did want to get it down on paper before we launched into the next five years.

Thanks, again, for everything.

Sincerely,

GOODWILL LETTERS TO NEIGHBORS

Your business may be about to do something that will irritate the people living or working in the neighborhood.

Perhaps you're going to enlarge your building, and this will entail some dust and noise. Or you may have to block off the street for a few hours each day while you remodel your warehouse driveway. Whatever the reason, you can help reduce the problem by letting your neighbors know in advance about (a) what you're planning to do, (b) why you're doing it, and (c) why it will be a good thing.

Dear Neighbor:

Starting in about two weeks, we're going to enlarge our warehouse. For about three weeks after that, there probably will be more construction noise than any of us is happy with, and I'm writing this letter in order to send you my apologies in advance.

We'll just about double the size of the interior by virtually filling up the entire block we now occupy.

The expansion is necessary because our business has done so well in the last four years that we need additional space in order to hold the increased inventory we require.

The workmen will be moving along as fast as possible. When they're through, we'll be able to serve our customers throughout the northeast much faster.

If you're inconvenienced in any way by the construction, please call Jim Holloway at 445-3879. He's in charge of fixing up any problems and will try to satisfy you at once.

Again, let me thank you for your understanding during this short period of building.

Sincerely,

REPLIES TO COMPLIMENTS

An excellent way to build goodwill is to reply promptly and pleasantly to all letters that you receive. In a previous chapter, we've discussed how to respond to complaint letters. Now, let's see about responding to complimentary letters. A pleasant and prompt reply can help solidify goodwill that you may have already created. Some basic principles of a good reply are:

First, thank the person for the letter.

Second, suggest that it's characteristic of the company.

Third, if the compliment refers to a specific person, mention that he or she will be told about the letters.

Fourth, repeat the thanks.

Here's an example of how these principles apply:

Dear Mrs. Ford:

Thank you for your lovely letter. I was delighted to hear that Mrs. Jacobson was so helpful to you.

Naturally, we hope that everyone who works for Cranwell's will be equally helpful. For, we know that this is the best way that we have of earning our customer's friendship and respect.

I'm sending a copy of your letter along to Mrs. Jacobson, and in our next employee meeting, I'm going to mention it as an example of the kind of attitude we should all try to cultivate.

Thank you again for writing. We'll do our best to continue to be as helpful to all our customers.

Sincerely,

12. Special Situations You Have to Handle

You may often be called on to handle special kinds of correspondence—correspondence a little out of the ordinary but, nevertheless, essential for the smooth running of a business. This includes business-related matters, such as letters of reference and letters of introduction, as well as matters that are only indirectly related to business, such as letters of condolence and congratulation. In this chapter, we'll discuss the principles involved in doing each of these well, and we will also provide many examples.

LETTERS OF REFERENCE

Organization

In general, most reference letters cover the following major points:

1. Explain the reason for the letter, if it isn't immediately obvious.
2. Explain your relationship to the person being written about: boss, colleague, customer, etc.
3. Mention how long you have known the person.
4. Describe the person's major qualifications. Usually, these will relate to (a) personal character and (b) business or professional qualifications.
5. If you feel it's appropriate, give an example of the person's qualifications.
6. Offer a general comment or recommendation.

Reference for an Employee

Here's a basic letter of recommendation which follows the suggestions given above:

Dear Mr. Johnson:

William Orne has asked me to send you a letter of reference on his behalf. I'm happy to do it.

Bill has been an assistant programmer with us for the past two years. During that time, he's worked exclusively in the accounting department. As his supervisor, I've had a chance to see him in operation on a daily basis.

He understands the basic principles of programming and knows how to apply them to almost any kind of accounting operation. He learns quickly and has always been highly self-motivated.

He works well with other people. He tends to be quiet and self-contained, but he has never failed to contribute ideas and goodwill in conferences and in undertaking new projects.

I can recommend him to a prospective employer without reservation.

Sincerely,

Writing a good letter of reference requires some careful attention to detail. If you're writing a reference letter in response to someone's request, make sure that your letter covers the information they've asked you for.

For example, if a friend or an employee asks you to write a letter of reference, ask him or her if there are any points they especially want emphasized. Make a note of them and mention them near the beginning of your letter.

Similarly, if you're writing a letter in response to an inquiry from an individual or an institution, notice what they're looking for. The chances are that they'll ask for specific kinds of information about abilities, interests, or qualifications; answer these items as specifically as you can.

Here are a couple of examples:

Reference for a Friend

You are sales manager of your company. A senior buyer for one of your good customers is planning to look for a new job in a different part of the country. She asks you to write her a reference letter which will describe her skill in negotiating good prices for first-quality merchandise.

Dear Sir or Madame:

Ms. Fran Carney has been buying menswear from our company for about five years. As the company's general sales manager, I've had close and regular contact with her during that time.

Ms. Carney has repeatedly proved herself to be highly skilled in negotiating good prices for first-quality merchandise.

She understands the needs of the marketplace, and she buys wisely and prudently. As a salesman, I naturally am always hopeful that her orders will be larger than they are; but as a businessman, I respect her fairness and the breadth of her knowledge.

As a case in point, last year she was one of the few buyers who correctly anticipated a shift away from leisure wear and toward more formal outfits. Her company profited handsomely.

If you're looking for a skilled professional, I think you need look no further than Ms. Carney.

Sincerely,

Reference for a Student

Here's another example. A young employee has decided to go to college and asks you to provide a reference. He gives you a form which the school has given him and asks you to fill it out. At the top of the form is the following statement:

The person whose name appears above has applied for admission to the University and has given your name as a reference. We are especially interested in your opinions about the following: learning ability, initiative and character—that is, the personal qualities which you feel are most outstanding.

If possible, please keep your letter less than one page long. We will appreciate hearing from you within the next 30 days. Thank you for your help.

Notice that the instructions ask for three kinds of information: learning ability, initiative, and character. In your letter, you'll emphasize those three qualities, if you can.

If you can't talk about them because you don't know about them, say so. And if you prefer not to talk about them because you can't say anything good, read further on, where we'll discuss ways to handle that problem.

Here, then, is one possible way a letter of reference to a university might be written. (If your letter were written on a form provided by the institution, you would probably eliminate the salutation and the first paragraph, and begin with the second paragraph.)

Gentlemen:

You ask for my opinions about John Smith, who has applied for admission to Bertram University.

For about five years, John has worked for me as a stock boy and delivery boy after school and during the summer. During that time, I've seen him grow into a splendid young man of excellent character. To answer your specific questions:

Learning ability: John has always shown an ability to learn quickly. He knows the names of scores of our customers, many of whom he's seen only once. He puts this knowledge to good use, addressing them by name when they come into the store. In that sense, he always helps build good-will for us.

Initiative: Because of the nature of his work here, he has virtually no chance to undertake independent projects in connection with his work. Consequently, I am unable to comment on that aspect of his abilities.

Character: John's most outstanding personal qualities are his honesty, his cooperativeness, and his good humor.

Much of our inventory is quite valuable and could easily be spirited away without immediate discovery. In all the years John has been with us, he has never given us any cause to doubt his complete honesty.

His cooperativeness has shown itself in his willingness to spend extra time at the store when we needed him—even when he had to give up other plans.

His good humor has always been evident, and he has made everyone who knows him feel better about life.

I believe that John will be a credit to any school, and I'm happy to be able to recommend him to you.

Sincerely,

Criticism in a Letter of Reference

When you're asked to write a reference letter for someone about whom you have doubts, there are a couple of ways to handle the problem. If your doubts are very strong, you might suggest to the person that you'd prefer not to write or that it might be more suitable if someone else wrote a letter.

Or, you might write a letter that clearly defines the limits of your recommendation.

Here are some examples:

If the person is willing but is not very careful about details:

> Mr. Smith is a willing worker. When he's involved in detailed work, we think that regular supervision will be helpful to him.

If the person is good at the job but has an abrasive personality:

> Mrs. Jones has always done a highly professional job. We've found that she's at her best when she's allowed to do her work with minimal distractions from fellow workers.

If the person tends to socialize too much with other workers, letting his or her own work slip by, but is otherwise able to do a good job:

> Mr. Gold does his work well. We've found that it's useful to him to have a clear schedule so that he can meet his regular deadlines.

In other words, when you need to criticize someone in a letter of reference and you don't want to be unfairly harsh, try to phrase your comments positively. Think in terms of: what does this person need in order to turn out good work?

LETTERS OF INTRODUCTION

A letter of introduction serves to introduce someone you know to other people you know. The letter may be addressed to a specific person or to a variety of people. The letter may be delivered in person by the one whom you're introducing or it may be sent.

A basic organization for a letter of introduction is:

1. Name the person you're introducing.
2. Explain his/her relationship to you or your firm.
3. Explain the reason for his/her visit.
4. Explain what you'd like the recipient of the letter to do.
5. Thank the recipient.

Here's an example of a letter of introduction which a company might send out in advance of a series of visits by a top executive.

> Dear Ms. Warren:
>
> John Mason, our vice-president of manufacturing, will be calling you within the next couple of weeks for an appointment.
>
> John is going on a one-month research trip around the country, looking into new manufacturing techniques that may be useful to us.
>
> We'll appreciate it if you can spend about an hour with him, explaining your newest equipment. If you can show it to him in operation, that will be even better.
>
> I'd like to thank you, in advance, for any help that you're able to give him.
>
> Sincerely,

The beginning of the letter will be changed a bit if the person being introduced is carrying it to the recipient:

Dear Jack:

This letter will introduce Harry Senour, our newest salesman.

Harry used to be in Chicago, with J. B. Morton, our toughest competitor, so he knows the business very well.

I've filled him in on your operation, and he has a good idea of what your needs are and how we can help you. In fact, he has a couple of interesting ideas that you might find productive.

Thanks for taking the time to see him. I think you're going to find him a very useful visitor.

Cordially,

LETTERS OF CONDOLENCE

Letters of condolence, usually sent to a family upon the death of a relative, should be brief and sincere. If the deceased is someone you've known for quite a while or someone who has meant a great deal to you, the letter may be somewhat longer.

Death of a Colleague

Dear Mrs. Peterkin:

Jim's passing is a great loss to all of us who have known him and worked with him.

We valued his experience and the generosity with which he shared his knowledge. Most of all, we valued his friendship; we shall all cherish the memory of his warmth and decency.

I send you my condolences, and I am joined by all of us who knew him. His memory will live with us for many, many years.

Sincerely,

Another Condolence Letter

Dear Mr. Weaver:

The loss of your mother grieves all of us at the office.

Over the years, she had become an essential part of our lives. She cheered us up more times than I can recall, and on frantic days, she somehow managed to share with us some measure of the calm which grew within her.

We want you to know that we have made an office collection in her memory and have donated the proceeds to the American Cancer Society.

We shall miss her, and yet, we are all better for having known her.

Sincerely,

Death of a Colleague's Relative

Dear Bill:

I was grieved to hear of your son's tragic accident.

Although I did not know him, I know how proud you were of him and what joy he gave you during his life.

My wife and I send you our sincere condolences.

Sincerely,

CONGRATULATORY LETTERS

There are innumerable occasions on which to send congratulatory letters: promotions, anniversaries, birthdays, special achievements, etc. While they're admittedly useful for business reasons, they also add a certain dimension—a purely human, noncommercial joy in another's good fortune.

In writing a congratulatory letter, consult your own good feelings: why are you happy to be writing it? What's the main feeling you want to convey?

Here are some sample letters that will help you to write your own.

Show Enthusiasm

If someone you know fairly well has received a substantial promotion and you're really happy for them, let your enthusiasm show through:

> Dear Mary:
> Congratulations! It couldn't have happened to a nicer person.
> When I read about your promotion, I had mixed feelings. First, I thought, "What a great company! They really recognize talent!" Then, I had another thought: "How come it took them so long to recognize *your* talent?"
> Finally, I decided to stop wondering about your company and just tell you how happy I am for you.
> I wish you all the luck in the world—and I know you're going to do a wonderful job.
>
> Regards,

Offer Support

A congratulatory letter may also contain an offer of support, as in this example of a letter to a new association president:

> Dear Mr. Anderson:
> We all know that the cream rises to the top. So, I guess it was nearly inevitable that you should become president of the Association.
> I'd like to add my congratulations to the many others you're receiving these days.
> They say that the age we're living in is cynical: that nobody believes in the virtues of hard work and commitment. "They" are obviously wrong—or at least, they haven't met you yet.
> I know that you have many plans and programs you're eager to initiate. If I can help you in any way, please call on me. I believe you can be the best president we've ever had, and I'll be delighted to help you achieve your goals.
> Again, I send you my best wishes for a most successful term.
>
> Sincerely,

For a Prize Winner

Here's a simple, all-purpose congratulatory letter that can be sent to virtually any-one who's won any kind of prize or position. Of course, you'll modify it to meet your particular circumstances. For example, you might substitute the word "I" for "All of us."

Dear Tom:

We were delighted to learn that you've won the annual Best Athlete award.

All of us are very proud of you—and we speak about your accomplishments with awe and admiration.

We send you our warm wishes for many more triumphs.

Cordially,

13. How to Write Effective Proposals

VIRTUALLY WITHOUT EXCEPTION, all proposals are like sales talks: they are an attempt to persuade someone to buy something or do something. In this sense, then, they are also like sales letters; and for this reason, it will be useful if you read Chapter 3 on sales letters in conjunction with this chapter.

We can divide proposals into two kinds: those for which there is fairly rigid format prescribed by the people to whom you're making the proposal, and those for which there is no rigidly prescribed format.

WHEN THE FORMAT IS PRESCRIBED

When the format is prescribed, it's obviously a good idea to study the requirements closely. *Pay particularly close attention to the technical requirements.* That includes the following points:

1. *Number of copies:* Do they ask for one copy or for more than one?

2. *Typographic format:* Do they specify the page size? Whether to single- or double-space? How wide the margins should be? Whether to write on one or both sides of the page?

3. *Topic headings:* If they suggest that you cover certain specific topics, be sure that those topics are headlined clearly in your proposal.

4. *Length:* If they suggest minimum or maximum lengths to parts of the proposal, or to the whole thing, be sure to observe them.

WHEN THE FORMAT IS NOT PRESCRIBED

When the format is not prescribed, your major task will be to make your report look good and be persuasive. These two requirements are quite distinct and are equally important. If your proposal looks bad, its persuasiveness will be diminished; if it's persuasive and it looks good, it will stand a better chance than an equally persuasive but poor-looking report.

Because appearance is so important, here are some suggestions to consider:

1. Use a good-looking cover. The more substantial your proposal, the heavier your cover should be. At the very least, use good quality letterhead paper. It will be more impressive if you use a simple cover. Check your stationery store: attractive, clear plastic bindings are available for less than a dollar. Thin cardboard bindings can also be bought for about the same price.

2. Use wide margins—at least 1½ inches on both sides.

3. Leave adequate margins at the top and bottom of the page—at least an inch.

4. Type on only one side of the sheet.

5. Double space throughout.

6. Start with a fresh sheet when you start a new section.

7. Use good quality white paper. Ask your stationery store for 20-pound rag bond—this has a good "feel." You might sample other papers which feel even heavier: they can help make even a mediocre report seem weightier.

8. Your proposal will undoubtedly be typewritten. No errors should show. Use correction fluid, chalk correction paper, or an eraser. And make sure your typewriter type is clean, so that the characters are sharp and clear. Your typewriter ribbon should be reasonably fresh, so that your characters are black and easily readable.

9. If possible, get copies of other proposals previously submitted to the place where you're submitting them. This will give you an idea of what's expected.

HOW TO ORGANIZE YOUR PROPOSAL

The left-hand column below gives general principles for organizing each section of a proposal. The right-hand column shows how the proposal itself might be worded.

Title: The title should clearly state what the proposal is about.

A Proposal for an Improved System for Training Computer Programmers

State the purpose of the proposal. It can be as brief as a sentence. Ideally, it should be no longer than one or two paragraphs.

This is a proposal to provide the Amer Corporation with a better system for training computer programmers. Its major difference from the present system will be that it uses outside contractors instead of the existing in-house staff.

Summarize the major benefits to be derived from the proposal.

The major benefits to be expected are: lower training cost, faster training, and decreased turnover.

Explain the major features of the plan.

Major Features of the System
The major features of the proposed new system are:
1. All new programmers will be trained by the outside contractors.
2. The contractors will bill the company a flat fee for each trainee.
3. The contractors will be responsible for holding refresher courses annually for all programmers.

Explain why this is an important idea. This section might mention the following facts: What's wrong with—or lacking in—the existing conditions? Why is this the right time to carry out your proposal? If you're suggesting a new committee or department or organization, are you sure it's necessary? This is the place to explain why. NOTE: If the people to whom your're making the proposal know little or nothing of what you're talking about,

Why This Proposal Is Needed
Over the past five years, the quality of our programmers has deteriorated steadily, while their salaries and fringe benefits have risen steadily.

Those in a position to understand the problem agree that the basic trouble lies with the staff trainers. We must eliminate them and find new trainers immediately if we expect to bring our programmers up to at least minimal standards.

it may be useful first to give them the background. In that case, you would start your proposal with this section, "Why This Proposal is Needed."

Then, you would put in a sentence that leads smoothly into the present first paragraph of the proposal. The sentence might be: "Therefore, we propose that the Amer Corp. adopt a new system for training computer programmers."

If your proposal is going to involve new people, or existing people in a new way, explain who they are and why they're the best ones for the job.

If you think it will be helpful, include résumés of the people you describe in this section. The résumés should be attached to the end of the report, as an appendix.

If your proposal is going to involve savings or expenditures, describe them in a separate section. If your financial figures are very detailed, it may be a good idea to simply summarize them here and to include a detailed analysis in an appendix.

The final paragraph is a call to action: it tells the reader what you want him or her to do or what decision you'd like to be forthcoming. Putting a deadline on the decision date may also help you to get an answer.

The system we recommend in this proposal solves all of our major problems, and we are unanimously in favor of it.

Who Will Be Involved in the New System

To administer the new system, it's suggested that a committee of three be established. They are: Bill Almly, vice-president of computer operations; Jack Jones, chief auditor; and Harriet Freedberg, personnel director.

We suggest these three because:

1. They are most directly concerned with upgrading the efficiency of the computer personnel.

2. They have already been working on the problem and are familiar with its nuances.

3. Their departments are most directly affected by the poor quality of our existing training. (See Appendix I for their résumés.)

What the New System Will Cost

Overall, we anticipate a saving of 10% to 20% at the end of the first year of operation under the proposed system. (Appendix 2 provides a complete cost analysis of the proposed system.) The proposed revisions will cost the corporation annually about $20,000 compared to the $18,000 now being invested in programmer training. However, this increase out-of-pocket expense will be more than offset by a decrease in errors and in turnover.

Where Do We Go from Here?

As soon as management approves this idea, the new Training Committee will go into action. They will plan on filing monthly progress reports with top management.

We would like to have a management decision by April 15, so that we can implement our plans with minimal delay.

OTHER POINTS TO THINK ABOUT

The people who read your proposal are probably going to be a little frightened by it because it suggests changing things from the way they've been done in the past. This, of course, is a completely natural reaction: no matter how much we may want new suggestions and ideas, we're often leery of them. So, if you're writing a proposal, what can you do to allay the doubts in the reader's mind?

One way is to ask yourself: if I were in the reader's shoes, what kinds of questions would I have? If you make up a list of these questions and provide answers in your proposal, you'll have increased the chances of acceptance.

Here's a discussion of some of the questions which the reader is likely to have.

1. *How competent are the people making the proposal?*

If the person to whom the proposal is being made knows the proposal writers, there's not much of a problem. But often, the reader doesn't know the proposer. So, it may be useful to give information about the background or the experience of the people involved in the proposal.

In the example given on the previous pages, résumés were included as an appendix. Consider whether additional information might be helpful. For example, if you're writing a proposal to another company, it may be helpful to include some letters from others praising you for past jobs. You might include these letters in an appendix, and you might refer to them near the beginning of your proposal—perhaps when you discuss who will be involved in carrying out the proposal.

2. *How practical and realistic is the proposal?*

Of course, the whole purpose of your proposal is to prove that what you're suggesting *is* practical. Nevertheless, the reader will have a number of doubts—especially if your idea is completely new. Here are some of the doubts likely to be present, and some suggestions about how to overcome them:

Is this the right time to do what the proposal suggests? If your reader is likely to ask this question, then you might answer it directly by including in your proposal a section titled. "Why the Time Is Right." In this section you can explain why it should be done now and what the consequences will be if it is not done now.

Is this proposal the right solution for the problem? Most business problems have several "right" solutions. If your reader is likely to ask whether a different proposal might be better, then you probably should deal with this in your proposal.

You may need to offer more explanations than are given in the sample proposal above. One way to handle this is with a section titled: "Some Solutions to the Problem." (In our sample proposal, we would put this section near the front, right after the "Major Benefits" section.)

A simple way of organizing this section is to discuss each of the alternatives briefly, then describe its advantages and disadvantages. From your description, it should be clear that the proposal you're suggesting is the best one.

Here's how such a section might be written for the sample proposal above:

Some Solutions to the Problem

The approach recommended in this proposal is one of several which we have considered. Those which seemed most sensible to us were:

1. Substantially upgrading the quality of the in-house training staff. The

advantage of this approach is that it would enable us to continue the training system we now have, but in a more effective manner. The disadvantage is that it would be quite costly: we estimated an increase of between $10,000 and $15,000 annually.

2. Contracting all company-operated computer services to an outside firm. The advantage of this approach is that it eliminates entirely the problem of training our own people. The disadvantages are several: we would lose direct control over our computer operations; we would have to drastically write down a considerable amount of expensive equipment, and the costs would be 20% to 30% higher than they now are.

3. A middle course between 1 and 2: keeping our in-house staff but contracting out the training. This is the course we are recommending in this proposal.

Are the people recommending it enthusiastic about it? A proposal that expresses enthusiasm engenders confidence. It's very much like a salesperson who's enthusiastic about the worth of a product: you tend to trust it and believe in it more than if it's put forward with indifference. In our sample proposal, this enthusiasm is suggested in a number of ways: it's in the title, which talks about an "improved system." It's in the first sentence, which mentions a "better system." It's expressed in the last sentence of the section "Why This Proposal Is Needed": "The system we recommend . . . solves all of our major problems, and we are all on record as being enthusiastically in favor of it."

Does the proposal suggest adequate staff and facilities for the job? If your proposal suggests setting up a new program that will involve a number of people and perhaps additional space or facilities, describe them in enough detail to show the reader that you've thought the problem through. The body of your proposal might simply describe the staffing in general terms, and you might go into considerable detail in an appendix.

3. *How important is the proposal to the company?*

The more important you can make the proposal seem to the well-being of the company, the more seriously it will be considered. In the sample proposal, this urgency is referred to in the section "Why This Proposal Is Needed." Among the questions a prospective reader will ask are:

Who'll benefit from the project—and in what way?
Will conditions improve measurably if it's successful?
Will we be worse off if it fails than if we had done nothing?

4. *Is it original and creative?*

Most people have mixed feelings about things that are new and creative. On the one hand, they like to be associated with creative projects because they're interesting and usually exciting, and they get talked about. On the other hand, they're risky: that which is new takes getting used to, and sometimes, it's hard to get used to new ideas without considerable discomfort. So, in writing your proposal, give some thought to the person who's going to make the final decision on whether to approve it. Is he or she likely to respond more favorably to something that's new and innovative or to something that's more conservative? Then, consider whether you can tilt your report accordingly.

Here are some examples of how you might slant a proposal in one direction or the other.

If you plan to suggest that your ideas are creative and original, you can introduce it with a paragraph like this:

> The problem we face is a severe one, and its solution demands bold and innovative thinking. Admittedly, it requires courage and persistence for any innovation to succeed. But we believe that our proposal is sufficiently creative to call forth the very best qualities of everyone who participates in it: once it's initiated, we are certain that it will be seen as natural, inevitable, and an immense improvement over the program it replaces.

On the other hand, if you want to suggest that your ideas, while creative and original, are also conservative and cautious, you might introduce them with a paragraph like this:

> Our idea adapts the best of the past to the new conditions we face today. Rather than abandon what has proved itself to be true and valuable, we have attempted to define its essence and give it new life and new meaning for the world we are moving into. For this reason, we think our proposal is eminently sound: it combines solid experience with an open-minded willingness to accept the future and to make the most of it. This approach has accounted for much of our success in the past, and we believe it is the correct approach for guiding us toward a successful future.

Some other points you might want to touch on in your proposal which relate to its originality and creativity:
 a. Does it duplicate or overlap other existing or forthcoming programs?
 b. Will it disturb or upset other existing or forthcoming programs?

5. *Is the budget soundly conceived?*
The soundness of your budget will be one of the most thoroughly scrutinized parts of your proposal. Ask yourself two questions:
 a. Is the budget adequate for the job I want to accomplish? And, is it obviously not so lavish that it appears wasteful?
 b. Does your budget include a contingency sum, in case expenses run higher than expected?

6. *Do you need to provide for evaluation of the project?*
It may help to make your proposal more persuasive if you include a section describing how you plan to evaluate the results of the project. Think about these things:
 a. How often should it be evaluated? Every month? Every six months? Once a year?
 b. What kinds of evaluation are needed: will you evaluate how well you've achieved specific objectives, how close you've come to general goals, how people feel about the project, or how the money has been spent?
 c. Who'll do the evaluating? Will it be an independent person or committee, or will it be people who are deeply involved in the project? In either case, you should be able to present a couple of good reasons explaining why these are the best people to do the job.

———————————— **HELPFUL HINT** ————————————

If you're making a proposal for a grant from a foundation, it is useful to know about The Foundation Center, which provides information on a variety of subjects relating to foundations. They publish a number of directories, and they also have free, short pamphlets available. Two that you may find helpful are: "What Will a Foundation Look for When You Submit a Grant Proposal?" by Robert A. Mayer, and "What Makes a Good Proposal?" by F. Lee Jacquette and Barbara L. Jacquette. The addresses of The Foundation Center are: 888 Seventh Avenue, New York, N. Y. 10019, and 1001 Connecticut Avenue, N.W., Washington, D.C. 20036.

14. How to Make Powerful Oral Presentations

THIS CHAPTER WILL tell you how to prepare any kind of spoken presentation that you plan to make to an audience. It could be for an audience of one, such as your boss, or for an audience of 1,000, such as at a convention or a sales meeting.

In either case, the essential points will be the same; only the details will vary.

In this chapter, we'll cover these four topics:

First, how to organize your ideas for a presentation.
Second, how to write the presentation.
Third, how to illustrate it.
Fourth, how to deliver it effectively.

ORGANIZING YOUR IDEAS

It will help you to organize your ideas better if you set up a chart like this:

	1	2	3
1. Who is the presentation addressed to? (name or brief job description)			
2. Attitude this person should have or action he/she should take when presentation is finished			
3. The most important thing to tell this person			
4. Second most important thing to tell this person			
5. Third most important thing to tell this person			

Question 1, "Who is the presentation addressed to?" is important because it helps you focus on your audience. There are three boxes to the right of the question because you might actually be talking to several people and/or groups of people in the audience. For example, if you were delivering a speech at a convention, you might be talking to your competitors, your boss, and your boss's boss. If you were delivering a report to a committee meeting, you might be talking to an engineer, a designer, and a marketing specialist. So, you'll answer Question 1 by entering the job titles of the most important people or groups of people in your audience.

Question 2, "Attitude this person should have or action he/she should take when presentation is finished," is important because in most cases, you'll want your audience to think or do something when you're finished. If you can write it down here, for each person or group you've listed after Question 1, you'll have gone a long way toward organizing your speech.

For example, do you want them to get out and sell harder; do you want them to appreciate your research; do you want them to follow a course of action you're recommending; do you want them to vote for a certain candidate? Your answers may be the same or different for each of the people or groups listed in Question 1. Be as ruthlessly honest here as you can, because the success of your presentation may depend largely on how accurately you answer this question.

Questions 3, 4, and 5 deal with the three most important things you can talk about to each person or group in your audience. By "important" I mean: what do you feel are the most important things you can tell them that will help them to have the attitude—or do the thing—you described in Question 2? Different people or groups in your audience may be moved by different kinds of information. Filling out this chart will enable you to see what information is most important for each of the groups you're talking to.

GETTING YOUR THOUGHTS TOGETHER

Once you've gone through the exercise of filling out the chart, you'll have a better idea of what to say. But you may still have a lot of information that needs to be organized in some logical way.

One way to get it organized is to talk into a tape recorder—without worrying about the order of importance or the logic of what you're saying. Just get it all on tape. Then, have your words transcribed. Make sure to have each sentence or idea start a new paragraph. This will make it much easier for you to organize your ideas when you move on to the next step. (Another way to achieve the same goal, if you can't use a tape recorder, is to write down your major facts on paper without worrying about organization. Again, each item should begin a new paragraph.)

Now, look at all your ideas. Number the most important ones "1," the next most important "2," and the least important "3."

Next, look at all your 1s, and use the alphabet to rank them in a rough order; that is, the most important will become 1a; the next most important 1b; the third will be 1c; and so on. Repeat the procedure for each of the remaining numbers.

As you do this, you'll find that some ideas are unimportant; eliminate them. Other ideas will say the same thing; combine them.

Another way to accomplish the same organizational format is to cut each of your paragraphs apart with a scissors, so that each piece of paper has one item. Then arrange them in categories, according to their importance. Once you've laid them out as you want them (it's nice to have a large area—a floor is often ideal), staple or tape them in their proper order to sheets of 8½×11 paper. You now have your basic presentation set up the way you want it.

HOW TO WRITE YOUR PRESENTATION

Every presentation, whatever its purpose and no matter how short it may be, needs a beginning, a middle, and an end.

The Beginning

In organizing your opening remarks, think about including these three topics:
1. Identifying yourself and your relation to the topic.
2. Describing what you're going to talk about.
3. Describing why it will benefit your audience to listen to you.

Identify yourself. If your audience knows your name and title, you can obviously forgo this step. But, if there are more than a couple of people in the audience who don't know you, tell them who you are and what your job is. Also, tell them why you're the one who's making this presentation. You might say something like this:

> I'm Liz Smith, head of the sales training department. One of my jobs is to chat personally with all new people and to explain how our department is organized.

Or,

> My name is Joe Jones, and I work in Maintenance Engineering. Our department has been working on the problem of lowering maintenance costs, and we've set up a committee to sift through all the ideas that have been suggested. As chairman of that committee, I'd like to tell you about what we've found.

Describe what you're going to talk about. You can usually do this in either one or two sentences:

> Today, I'd like to discuss new product marketing.

> For the next 30 minutes, I'd like to focus your attention on better ways to service your oil burners.

Describe why it will benefit your audience. This is one of the most important things you can tell them, because everyone wants to know: "What's in it for me?" Among the things you might say are:

> It's an important subject because we've made a number of changes which will help put more money in your pocket.

> What I'm going to explain will help you to do your jobs more quickly and efficient.

> This new information will enable you to plan your estate with more confidence and with a better chance of raising your post-retirement income.

The Middle

Once you've finished the beginning of your presentation, you'll be ready to go into the middle, where you deliver the bulk of your information.

It may be helpful to make a transitional statement, indicating that you're leaving the beginning and going into the middle. Here are some simple, straightforward transitional sentences:

> Perhaps the best way to begin is by giving you some background: how did we arrive at the point we're at today?

> In order to understand this whole subject, it's a good idea to begin at the beginning.

> As a starting point, let's begin with the directive that Mr. Jones issued recently.

Once you've made the transition, you're ready to design the major section of your presentation. And here, you'll follow the outline you've prepared. If your outline consists simply of a few key words and you want to write it all out in sentence form, there are a couple of ways to do it easily. One is to use your outline as a guide while you talk the presentation into your tape recorder. Then, play the tape recorder back two or three times. Don't try to make any judgments the first time through: simply listen for the general impression your ideas make. The second or third time through, make notes in the margins of your outline—notes about changes or deletions or additions.

Now, try to write the speech as you spoke it. Double space and leave plenty of room in the margins, so that you can make changes later.

If you don't have a tape recorder, try talking out loud from your notes two or three times. By the third time, you'll know pretty well what changes you want to make. The fourth time, write down what you'd like to say.

Still another way is simply to write your presentation from your outline, without reciting it aloud. Some people find this easier. If you run into trouble getting started, skip the start and go on to the first section you find easy to write.

As you write, it's a good idea to let your audience know each time that you're starting a new major point. For example, your transitional sentence leading to the middle might be:

> Now, I'd like to discuss the first of the three major points I'm going to talk about today.

When you finished that point, you might say:

> That concludes our discussion of the first point. Now, let's talk about the second point.

When you've finished the second point, you might say:

> So much for the second point. Let's turn now to the third and final point.

And when you've finished the third point you might say:

> And that concludes my third major point.

THE END

The concluding idea in your presentation can serve either or both of the following functions.

First, it can review the highlights of your presentation. If you've made several points which you feel need to be reemphasized, cover them briefly at the conclusion.

> To repeat my major points: first, we need more recreation space in the town; second, there is only one likely area that we can obtain—the Mason property; third, we should decide tonight to go ahead with the purchase.

Second, your conclusion can be a call to action, or it can argue for a point of view that you want your audience to take:

> I think the facts point to one obvious conclusion: we need to make a decision immediately. If we wait a week longer, our opportunity will slip by. And it will not come again. If my arguments make sense to you, then I urge you to vote now—vote yes or no—but let's do it at once.

───────────── **HELPFUL HINT** ─────────────

Match your beginning and your conclusion. At the beginning of your presentation, you explained what you were going to talk about and why it was important to your audience. It will give your presentation a feeling of completeness if you refer back to that point at the conclusion. For example, suppose that in your opening remarks you said:

> **We're going to learn how our office filing system works. The sooner you understand it, the easier your job will be.**

Your conclusion might use similar words:

> **That's a review of how the office filing system works. We want you to understand it, because we want to make your job easier.**

HOW TO ILLUSTRATE YOUR PRESENTATION

Good, clear pictures and charts can help almost any speech. Conversely, poor ones can hurt a speech. Here are some suggestions for using visuals to enhance your presentation.

First, there are many different techniques available. Those in most common use are discussed below.

Flipcharts. Flipcharts may be blank pads of paper on which you write your main points or draw diagrams as you speak, turning to a fresh page each time you want to change the message. Or, you may prefer to write out your main points ahead of time, so that as you talk, you merely turn the pages. For more elaborate presentations or for those which will be delivered many times, you may want something more durable than paper. Cardboard and plastic flipcharts are also available. The size should be appropriate to the number of people in your audience. If you're going to be talking to one person sitting at a desk, you may want a small chart, one that measures about one-by-two feet, that can easily be set up on the desk. For an audience of up to 50 people, you can obtain flipcharts as large as five feet long. The important thing is that the chart be large enough for the audience to see your writing clearly.

Slides. Slides are useful for audiences of one up to several thousand. However, they lose clarity in a well-lit room. This means that to get full benefit from your slides, you'll have to dim the lights. The most popular-size slide is the rectangular 35mm: this fits standard slide projectors. Superslides are also popular: they have the same outside dimension as 35mm slides, but the frame is narrower and the picture area is larger. Your presentation will look smoother and more professional if all your slides have the same layout, so don't mix superslides with 35mm. And if you use all 35mm, try to have them all horizontal, or all vertical.

Demonstration boards. These are usually rigid boards with a surface that holds movable letters, pictures, designs, etc. The items can be easily moved or removed by the speaker. Flannel boards have been popular for years. More recently, Velcro boards have become popular. Velcro is a special fabric of microscopic loops. Objects to be placed on Velcro board have a different kind of Velcro—one with microscopic hooks that hold onto the loops until peeled off—glued to their backs. A third board is magnetic—and magnetic strips are fastened to the object to be mounted on the board. The fourth "board" is the chalkboard, which is now rarely used in presentations unless the room is equipped with it. Then, of course, it may be used very much like a flipchart on which you write as you speak.

Overhead projectors: Overhead projectors are designed to be used by the speaker, who can add overlays to make progressive disclosure of information. A major advantage of the overhead projector is that the speaker can write on the drawing while talking—which often helps add informality and liveliness to the talk. (They're called "overhead" projectors because the material to be projected is placed on a horizontal surface through which a bright line shines upward to an angled mirror which shoots it at the screen in front of the audience.) Overhead projectors are large, and tend to be awkward to carry around.

Other materials. Filmstrips, motion pictures, and recordings are also used in presentations. However, they involve extensive and relatively expensive technical preparation.

DESIGNING YOUR VISUALS

Perhaps the most important single point that can be made about visual support is that it should be simple, clear, and immediately obvious to your audience. If you're writing your important points on an easel as you go along, this will be fairly easy to accomplish, because you'll usually write only a small amount and then speak about it. The rule should also be followed when you're using slides or any other visual support that's been prepared in advance of your talk.

As a general rule, put no more than two or three words on a slide. If you keep it down to a few words, everyone in your audience will immediately understand what you mean. The more words you add, the longer it will take the audience to understand and the more chance there is for confusion.

How do you select only two or three words? Simply look at your paragraph and put down the most important words in it. Then, rigorously pare, pare, pare. Eventually, you'll have your idea down to a bare minimum. Don't worry about not having a complete sentence. In most cases, you don't want a complete sentence: you want merely a key phrase to remind the audience of what you're talking about and to alert them when you begin to talk about something new.

Here are a couple of examples. The words in capital letters on the left are the words that appear on the slide. The words on the right are the opening remarks of a speech.

Example 1

DOCUMENT CREATION— AN OVERVIEW	Document creation—the subject on which I'm going to focus for the next 20 minutes—has been of intense interest to humanity for several thousand years, starting, I guess, with the Ten Commandments.

Example 2

SERVICE STATIONS— THE LEADER	We are convinced that service stations should sell more tires than any other kind of retail outlet.
MORE PROSPECTIVE CUSTOMERS	First, we see prospective customers regularly—about once a week. That's more often than any other tire merchant. So, we have the first shot at solving the customer's needs.
MORE SALES SUPPORT	Second, we have more sales support than any other tire merchant. This includes point of sale materials, co-op advertising, and a competitive tire line.

You may have a number of related ideas that you want the audience to keep in mind. Instead of putting them all on a single slide, put the first idea on one slide; then when you discuss the second idea, show a new slide with your first idea and the new one; then when you come to the third idea, change to a third slide with the first two ideas plus the third one. For example:

1. GET ORGANIZED	A successful drug promotion is made of four key elements. First, get organized.
1. GET ORGANIZED 2. SALES ATMOSPHERE	Second, create a selling atmosphere.
1. GET ORGANIZED 2. SALES ATMOSPHERE 3. COMMUNICATE THE PROMOTION	Third, communicate the promotion to the public and to your own people.
1. GET ORGANIZED 2. SALES ATMOSPHERE 3. COMMUNICATE THE PROMOTION 4. ASK FOR THE ORDER	And fourth, ask for the order.

Your presentation will flow more smoothly if you maintain a fairly steady rhythm in visual changes. This is especially true of slide presentations. If you're giving a 15 minute speech, and bunch all your slides in the first three or four minutes, then make no changes at all for the next five or six, and then have a flurry at the end, you'll create a less professional effect than if you were to make one or two slide changes every couple of minutes.

If your slide presentation doesn't require any slide changes for a prolonged period, it will create a more professional appearance if, instead of turning off the slide projector, you leave on a single general-purpose slide—perhaps your company's logo.

When presenting charts or diagrams, follow the same principle. A graph with a single line is often easier to follow than one with two or more lines. If you want to contrast two trends on a graph, ask yourself whether your audience will follow it more easily if you show it with only one line first, then after explaining it, add a second line.

HOW TO DELIVER YOUR PRESENTATION EFFECTIVELY

Effective public speaking is most easily learned by practice. But there are a few simple technical things you can do to improve your speaking style, even if you're making your first public presentation.

First, rehearse, rehearse, rehearse. Get your family and your friends to listen to you. Have them make critical notes while you're talking: were there words they didn't understand; did you speak too softly; was your voice monotonous?

Second, make sure that the copy you're reading from is clear and legible. Some people have their speeches typed on a typewriter with type about 1 times the size of a regular typewriter's. This makes the speech much easier to see.

Third, make helpful notes to yourself in the margins: remind yourself of where to pause, or where to look up at the audience. Both pausing and looking up are enormously important in making an effective presentation; they help the audience feel that you're *talking* rather than *reading* to them.

Fourth, if you're using visuals, note on the script what each one is supposed to say. If you plan to write certain points on an easel pad, you might jot them down on the margin. (Professional speechwriters usually type the entire speech on the right half of the page only, leaving the left half blank for entering special notes or information about slides.)

Fifth, avoid turning your head to look at each slide. Turning around is the mark of the nervous amateur, and it tends to make the audience feel that the speaker is unreliable. Of course, if you're referring to some specific feature on the slide, naturally you'll point to it. Even then, don't talk at the screen: keep as much of your body as possible turned to the audience. Turn your head to the screen only when it's necessary.

Sixth, observe professional speakers. Television spokesmen can provide a number of useful tips: watch how they look directly at the camera—they're not really looking directly at you, but they seem to be doing exactly that; you can do the same thing by looking directly at some member of your audience periodically. Remember also to smile occasionally: your audience is your friend—if you'll let it be.

15. How to Write Persuasive Résumés

YOUR RÉSUMÉ IS a sales message: if it's effective, it will arouse enough interest in the buyer—your prospective employer—for him or her to consider you for a job. As with any sales message, it will be more effective if it's clear, to the point, and easily understandable.

Here's a sample résumé. There's nothing sacred about this format, but it's simple and easy to follow, if you want to adapt it. (The numbers in parentheses refer to the numbered paragraphs following the résumé.)

(1)   Thomas G. Williamson
310 Madison Avenue
Cromwell, Pa. 55555
(123) 456-7890

(2)   Résumé

(3) 1972 — Present: **(4)** Chief Purchasing Agent
(5) Cromwell Electronic Corp.
Cromwell, Pa.

(6) I am responsible for purchasing for all departments of this company, which manufactures a wide range of electronic parts for systems control equipment. I supervise a staff of three.

(7)   Having been in this position for four years, I have an extremely broad knowledge of the most reliable and efficient electronic suppliers in the western industrial world, and I am on first-name terms with many of the leading firms' top executives. I can usually obtain urgently needed materials quickly and at the lowest possible cost.

1970 — 1972:   Purchasing Department
Carver Moldings Co.
Haddonville, W. Va.

During this period, I was promoted from foreman to purchasing manager—the highest position in the purchasing department.

(8)   My responsibilities included negotiating contracts with a wide variety of suppliers, making regular reports to top management, and suggesting and implementing methods for decreasing purchasing costs.

1966—1970:   Hourly worker
Centerville Manufacturing Co.
Dayson, Fla.

As an assembly-line worker, I gained an appreciation of the importance of quality control. This experience has helped me, as a purchasing agent, to analyze potential suppliers on the basis of quality as well as price.

Education

(9)   College: Dayson Community College
Dayson, Fla.
B.A., 1966

Technical/
Professional: Purchasing Agents Association
Summer Training Program
New York, N.Y.
1972, 1974, 1976

High School: Dayson High School
Dayson, Fla.
1960—1964

Service Record

1964—1966:   U.S. Army
Honorable Discharge as Technical Sergeant

Personal

(10)   Marital Status: Married, 3 children
Health: Excellent
Height: 5'10"
Weight: 165

Honors and Associations

(11)   1975:   Purchasing Agent of the Year Award, Pennsylvania, Purchasing Agents Association; Member, National Association of Purchasing Agents; Member, Electronic Buyers of America; President, Cromwell Presbyterian Men's Association.

References

(12)   Available on request.

ANALYSIS OF THE RÉSUMÉ

1. Place your name, address, and telephone number at the top of the page, where they're immediately visible. You can put them in the middle or on the left or right side.

2. "Résumé" is one possible title. You might prefer others, such as "Work Experience," "Summary of Work History," or "Professional Experience." Some people use no title.

3. A chronological arrangement is usually the easiest and most logical way to organize your working experience. Put your most recent job first and then move back to earlier jobs. When you date your first entry, use "Present" rather than the current year; this will let the prospective employer know that you are now employed.

4. List your job title before you mention your company. The reason: a prospective employer is probably going to be more interested in what you do than in whom you work for. Don't lie, but if the opportunity is open to you, give yourself the best-sounding title you can think of that describes your job.

5. It's optional whether you put down an employer's street address. Listing the town where the firm is located gives a realistic tone.

6. Summarizing your job is often difficult, but it may be the most important part of your résumé. So, think about it carefully. These ideas will help:

Is there a written job description of your responsibilities? You might adapt it for your résumé. It may make your job look even more important than you think it is.

Another idea: what does the person who's likely to hire you want in a new employee? Experience? Reliability? A good personality? Whatever it is, stress that element in the summaries of all your jobs, if it's at all possible. In this résumé, for example, both the first and second job descriptions mention that the applicant knows a wide variety of suppliers; evidently, he feels this is important to a prospective employer. All of your past jobs may not fit this mold, but you can probably find something in all of them that will be of interest to a prospective employer. For example, in this case, the applicant's first job was working on an assembly line—probably a boring, pointless job. But he extracted from it the fact that it gave him an appreciation of quality, which stands him in good stead as a purchasing agent.

Make each job sound different from the others. A prospective employer usually isn't as interested in someone who's done the same job repeatedly in different places as in someone who's had a variety of experiences that will all help the applicant to do a better job. For example, if you're a mechanic, can you emphasize your experience on trucks in connection with one job, on sedans with another, and on sports cars with still another?

7. Don't boast, but let the prospective employer know about your accomplishments. In the sample résumé, the fact that this applicant is on a first-name basis with many large suppliers is a feather in his cap. You can often think of some honor that your group has received or some element that sets you apart from the run-of-the-mill applicant. Here's the place to use it.

8. Put your best foot forward. You may be able to make even a simple job sound more glamorous by using your imagination. In this résumé "negotiating contracts" may simply mean sending out letters to ask manufacturers if they carry certain items; "making regular reports to management" may mean that invoices were routinely sent upstairs to the boss; and "suggesting . . . methods for decreasing purchasing costs" may mean that he started ordering certain items in wholesale lots. The moral is: always tell the truth in your résumé, but don't be afraid to show the truth in its best light.

9. Mention all the schools you've attended and the degrees you've earned. If you've earned none, put down the dates of attendance.

10. Most personal data is optional, and employees are not usually required to include it. However, some people like to put it in if it reflects positively on them. For example, this applicant felt that his being married and the father of three children gave him an appearance of stability.

11. This is a general heading under which you can stuff almost any subject that fits, but doesn't fit elsewhere. If you belong to brotherhoods, fraternities, social clubs, or anything else that you're proud of, this is the place to put it in. A word of caution: if you think that some of your affiliations may raise questions in a prospective employer's mind, consider whether or not to include them. There are two sides to the question. On the one hand, you may feel that if an employer refuses to consider you because of your affiliations, you're better off not working there. On the other hand, if you're really hungry for the job, you may unnecessarily be hurting your chances of getting it.

12. If your references are famous or very well known in your industry or in the community where you're applying for a job, it may be a good idea to list their names and addresses here. Otherwise, give them if you're asked during an interview.

OPTIONAL INFORMATION

At the top of your résumé, under your name, you may want to briefly mention what kind of a job you're looking for. You might put: "Job Objective: Administrative Assistant" or "Position Desired: Maintenance Engineer."

If you do this, it will let your prospective employer know immediately what kind of position you're seeking, which is an advantage. On the other hand, listing your objective may eliminate your being considered for other jobs for which you might be well qualified. Perhaps the best course of action is to consider your situation very carefully and to think about what *you'd* do if you were the prospective employer reading your résumé. Would a "Job Objective" title be helpful or not? If you have any doubt, it is safer to omit the heading. You can always insert it in a covering letter or memo.

———————————— **HELPFUL HINT** ————————————
It's probably better not to mention your present or past salary, or the salary you'd like to get. If the salary offered is less than you want or have been getting, the employer may disqualify you for asking too much. If the salary offered is more than you expect or have been getting, the prospective employer is less likely to mention it to you. Have a clear idea of what you want, but don't mention it until you're asked about it.

ABOUT STYLE

When you describe your activities, you'll probably select one of the three most common styles. You'll write in the first person:

I worked as a research associate.

Or, you'll write in the third person:

He worked as a research associate.

Or, you'll use no personal pronouns:

Worked as a research associate.

Select the one you feel most comfortable with: any one of them is acceptable if it's used consistently and correctly. However, do be aware of these points.

When you use the first person style, try to use as few "I's" as possible. When you use too many of them, they can make you sound egotistical.

The third person style can sound dreadfully pretentious if it gets to be boastful. So, if you use this style, be modest.

If you use no personal pronouns however, your language may sound too telegraphic and robotlike.

The best course, whatever style you select, is to read aloud what you've written. If it sounds all right to your ears, it will probably sound all right to the prospective employer, as well.

A RÉSUMÉ BASED ON SKILLS

Some employers are most interested in the kinds of experience you've had in the past few years, and you may want to write a résumé which organizes your material accordingly. Instead of following a strict chronological order, as the previous résumé does, each paragraph will describe a different skill you've mastered or a different assignment you've handled. This kind of résumé may be particularly useful if you've spent a considerable amount of time working for one company in a variety of jobs.

To organize such a résumé, think first about the kind of job you'd like to get and what qualifications are required for it.

Then, when you write your paragraphs, list first those jobs that bear most closely on the work you want to do.

For example, let's say that you're a chemist and you'd like a job as a sales representative for a chemical company. Think of the qualifications that a sales representative should have: an ability to work with people, to be a self-starter, to be a good planner, to have some degree of skill at communications.

You might write some paragraphs like these:

> During the past six years, I have carried out varied assignments for my department. They have required me to exercise a number of sales and marketing skills. Some typical examples:
>
> **The ability to work with people.** For a period of six months, I worked with a team of researchers from four of our foreign subsidiaries in adapting American formulas to their local communities. The project was completed well within deadlines, and the products are now being introduced successfully overseas.
>
> **The ability to be a self-starter.** I have suggested a number of research projects which I felt would be beneficial to the company. In one case, the project resulted in a new line of solvents, which have provided a profitable new source of income.
>
> **Planning skills.** During the past two years, I have been in charge of planning the schedules and budgets for about six major projects. The work has involved both cost analysis and PERT programming. In every case, we have stayed within the limits of our time and money budgets.

Communications skills. On the average, I write about six major reports a year on various aspects of my projects. These aspects include technological reviews, personnel reports, and marketing possibilities. A number of those reports have been adapted by the field sales force as an aid in making their sales presentations more effective.

─────────────── HELPFUL HINT ───────────────

Talk about results. People like to get close to a winner, and if you can show that your work has benefited your colleagues or superiors, you'll be much more desirable as a prospective employee. For example, in the paragraphs preceding this Helpful Hint, the results are mentioned frequently. The paragraph on ability to work with people mentions that the products are now being successfully introduced; the paragraph on being a self-starter talks about the profitable new source of income that the applicant suggested.

COVERING LETTERS

A covering letter that you send along with your résumé usually should emphasize *not* that you're enclosing a résumé but that the recipient will be very interested in the information in the résumé. In other words, the covering letter is—or should be—a sales letter for the résumé. Here are a few examples that you can adapt to your needs.

The best time to send a résumé is before you have to look for a job. Here's an example. Notice that the letter talks as much about the prospective employer as about the letter writer—always a good idea in any business letter.

Dear Mr. Jacobson:
    Because of your school's reputation for exceptionally high teacher standards, I'm sending you my professional résumé.
    As you'll notice, I've been teaching in a school whose philosophy is quite similar to yours. The experience has been a happy one for me, and I expect to make my career in the kind of educational institution in which you are involved.
    I plan to move to your area within the next six months. After my arrival, I plan to call you for an appointment to see if you might have a staff opening in the near future.

                                                            Sincerely,

Here's a model letter sent after the writer has met the recipient. It tells the recipient that the writer is interested in a new opportunity, if the right one comes along. Notice that the writer talks about phoning the recipient. If you feel less aggressive, you might write instead: "Call or write me when you'd like to chat. I'll be happy to exchange ideas with you."

Dear Ms. Jespers:
    When we met at the Boutique Show last week, you asked me to send you a résumé of my working experience. Here it is.
    While I'm happy with my present work, I'm naturally interested in new opportunities that promise more challenge and reward.
    I'll plan on calling you in about a week to ten days to see if you'd like to get together.

                                                            Sincerely,

16. How to Select and Buy Stationery and Letterheads

You CAN MAKE a favorable impression on your customers if you think carefully about the kind of stationery you use.

This doesn't mean that the stationery has to be expensive. One of the most striking business envelopes I've seen was a standard, commercial type with no printing on it. But, the sender of the letter was an expert penman, and his beautiful handwriting immediately suggested integrity, quality, and reliability—three characteristics that happened to be very important in this person's business.

THINKING ABOUT WHAT YOU NEED

Before buying business stationery, think about what you'll need. If you write a lot of fairly long letters, you may need $8\frac{1}{2} \times 11$ paper, which is the standard size of a full sheet. However, if most of your correspondence tends to be brief, you may save money by ordering smaller stationery— 7×10 or even less.

SOME FACTS ABOUT PAPER

Here, you may learn more than you want to know about paper. On the other hand, if you're a business person, sooner or later you'll probably be involved in buying stationery, brochures, or paper in one of its many forms. The information which follows will give you at least a speaking acquaintance with some basic facts you ought to have.

Paper is usually defined by the use to which it's put. The most common grades are:

Bond. Bond is the paper most often used for letters and business forms. It takes ink well and can be erased easily.

Coated. Coated papers have smooth glossy coatings. They are used for high printing quality. There are many varieties: coated on one or both sides, dull coated, etc.

Text. Text papers have attractive textures and colors. They are used for booklets, announcements, and special purposes.

Book. Less expensive than text papers, book papers are used mostly for books.

Offset. Offset is similar to book paper, but it is treated to resist the moisture present in offset printing.

Cover. Cover papers are heavier weights of coated and text papers. They are often used as covers for booklets. In addition, some papers are made exclusively for covers.

Index. Index paper is stiff and receptive to ink.

Newsprint. Newsprint paper is used for newspapers.

Tag. Often used for printing tags, tag paper may be printed on one or both sides. It bends and folds well.

HELPFUL HINTS

Most printing papers are identified by "basis weight." This is the weight of 500 sheets—one ream—of the paper in its basic size. (The basic size differs for different grades. The basic size of a sheet of bond paper is 17" × 22"; the basic size of a sheet of newsprint is 24" × 36."

The greater the weight of the paper, the heavier each individual sheet, and usually, the better it feels in the hand. In writing papers, 20-pound rag bond is a good quality and has a good feel.

KNOW YOUR ENVELOPES

Your stationery store can supply you with a dizzying variety of regular and special envelopes, each style coming in many sizes. Here are the basic styles and their uses.

Commercial. Commercial envelopes are used for most business and for statements.

Window. Window envelopes are used mainly for invoices and statements. They save time in addressing and eliminate the possibility of typing the wrong address on the envelope.

Self-sealing. Self-sealing envelopes have upper and lower flaps which have adhesive that seals without water, thus saving time.

Open-side. Open-side envelopes are good for direct mail and periodicals. Absence of seams permits good-looking front and back printing.

Baronial. Baronial envelopes are similar to open-side envelopes. They are used for announcements, invitations, etc.

Bankers flap. Bankers flap envelopes are for very bulky material. The paper is much stronger than ordinary commercial envelopes.

Wallet flap. Wallet flap envelopes are like bankers flap envelopes; they hold a great deal and are made of strong paper.

Clasp. Clasp envelopes are used for carrying bulky correspondence safely. They are strong, and they can be opened and closed many times.

String-and-button. String-and-button envelopes are similar to clasp envelopes.

Open-end. Open-end envelopes have wide seams and gummed flaps to protect their contents under rough handling. Widely used for mailing reports, catalogs, magazines, booklets, etc.

Expansion. Expansion envelopes have pleated sides, which enable them to expand as more material is inserted in them.

SELECTING YOUR LETTERHEAD

Your printer or stationer will be able to show you books of sample letterheads, which you can adapt to your business.

One of the first things to think about is the information you want to put on your letterhead. Certainly, the name of your company, your address, and your telephone number are essential. But then consider: might you want to put on more than one address; more than one telephone number? Also, what about the names of any individuals: if you're the president, do you want your name on it? Or if you're selecting letterheads for a committee, do you want their names to appear?

Also, you might want to have your letterheads match your business cards. If your cards are distinctive or have special artwork, your printer may be able to transfer the design to your letterhead.

When you're in doubt, select a simpler rather than a more elaborate design. For example, some letterheads place the company's address on the bottom of the sheet. It often looks quite good, but it requires an alert typist. If you write long letters, you're apt to run the typed lines too close to the address, ruining the appearance of the page.

If you prefer an original letterhead design, retain the services of a commercial artist who's had considerable experience in lettering. A local advertising agency or commercial artist can often do the job for you; check the Yellow Pages of your telephone book if you don't know any artists. Tell them what you're interested in, find out the price for (a) four or five sketches from which you can select what you want, and (b) finished artwork, ready for printer. If possible, get estimates from two or three sources.

THE PRINTING POSSIBILITIES

You can select one of several kinds of printing for your letterhead.

The most expensive is engraving, which produces a raised design on the paper. The raised portion may be printed, or it may be left unprinted. It's the most expensive method of printing, and it also looks the most luxurious.

Another kind of printing, called thermographic or electrostatic printing, creates a raised type. It is similar to engraving but less expensive. You can usually have it with a shiny finish or a dull one: check with the printer to see if you can get what you like.

Letterpress is a type of printing frequently used by commercial job printers. Letterpress produces a sharp, clear impression.

Offset printing is usually the least expensive. A good offset letterhead can be nearly as crisp and sharp as a good letterpress job. A poor one can be abominable. Usually, you get what you pay for in printing, so be sure to see samples of other work the printer has done before you commit your job.

ENVELOPES

You'll probably want your stationery and your envelopes to match. Usually, your printer will submit a price that includes printing both. One word of caution may prevent dissatisfaction: to cut corners, a printer may use the same type on the envelope as on the stationery. If the print size is appropriate, there may be nothing wrong with it.

But, you may want a different type size on the envelope—often an envelope's type should be smaller because the printing surface is smaller. Find out in advance exactly what the printer plans to put on the envelope.

SAMPLE LETTERHEADS

While sample books of stationery can provide you with many standard letterheads, you may want some fresh ideas about what you can do with your own. Here are some samples.

17. Making Your Letters Look Good

THE APPEARANCE OF your letter on the page can make your message look either weak and amateurish or strong and well organized. In general, strive for an appearance of simplicity, neatness, and balance. Leave generous margins on all sides. If you make typing errors, correct them invisibly with correction fluid, correction paper, or neat erasures. Simply crossing out the error makes your letter look sloppy.

On this page and the next are models of two business-letter styles. They are both in common use and will serve as guides in the preparation of your own letters.

WILLIAMSON TELEVISION CO.
47 Maple Boulevard
Appleton, New York 12345

(1)   **(A)**   February 14, 19____

                                      (B)

(2) Miss Thea Peabody, Manager
Master Rubber Co.
6783 Longwood Avenue
Whitby, North Dakota 56789

                                      (C)

(3) Dear Miss Peabody:

                                      (D)

You recently asked us to explain our new policy of guaranteeing all television sets for five years.

The guarantee is as good as it sounds. At no charge, we will repair or replace any damaged or defective part of your television set for a period of five years after you buy it at our store, if you agree to bring the set in for diagnosis and repair.

(4)   We're able to make this offer because we find that the cost of house calls accounts for more than half of our labor expenses. By eliminating that cost, we are able to guarantee our customers the thing they are most interested in: years of no-cost repair service.

You'll find, we think, that no other store in this area offers a similar guarantee. It is one more exclusive service that we're able to give our customers. If you'll call us or drop by the store, I'll be glad to explain some of the other advantages of buying your next television set from us.

(E)

(5)   **(F)** Sincerely,

(6)   **(G)**

(7)   **(H)**   Roberto Williamson, President

(8) pcr

(I)

(9) Enc.

ANALYSIS

(1) Date line

(2) Address

(3) Salutation

(4) Body of letter

(5) Complimentary close

(6) Signature

(7) Typed name and official title

(8) Reference: initials of typist

(9) Enclosures

(A) Dateline flush right

(B) 4 line spaces (3 lines blank)

(C) Double space

(D) Double space

(E) Double space

(F) Start at center of paper

(G) 4 line spaces (3 lines blank)

(H) Double space

(I) Double space

VERNON WALLER, INC.
Contractors-Builders
Anderson Plaza
Anderson, Florida 09876
Telephone: (432) 234-4320

(1)   May 24, 19____   **(A)**

         Mr. Robert Gordon Tregg   **(B)**
(2)   45 Sixth Avenue
         Ardmore, California 90867
                                      (C)

(3)   Dear Mr. Tregg:

         Thank you for giving us the opportunity to bid on the house you're planning to build in Anderson.

Making Your Letters Look Good 107

Our bid for the entire house is $60,000.

(4) This includes: excavation for the foundation and building of the house; all electrical, plumbing, and heating work; construction of the fireplace and chimney; and disposal of surplus earth after construction is finished and the land has been graded.

On the enclosed sheets, you'll find a detailed analysis of our bid.

We were very impressed with your plans, and we would be pleased and proud to work on the home and to build into it all of the quality and care that you would if you were building it yourself.

If you have any questions, please call me, and I'll do my best to answer them.

(D)

(5) Sincerely,

(6)   **(E)**

(7) Vernon Waller, Jr.
President

(F)

(8) sd

(9) Enc.   **(G)**

ANALYSIS

(1) Date

(2) Letter address

(3) Salutation

(4) Body

(5) Complimentary
close

(6) Signature

(7) Typed name and title

(8) Reference:
Initials of typist

(9) Enclosure indication

(A) 4 line spaces
(3 lines blank)

(B) Double space

(C) Double space

(D) Double space

(E) 4 line spaces
(3 lines blank)

(F) Double space

(G) Double space

18. How to Research Like a Pro

As a business person, your need for reliable facts is essential to the successful conduct of your business. If you're lucky, you'll have those facts at hand. But, from time to time, you may have to dig up information from new sources. And you may wonder about where to get it and how to do your research most efficiently. Here are some suggestions that may be helpful.

BEFORE YOU LOOK, THINK

The first necessity of good research is to know, as precisely as possible, what you're looking for. So, on a sheet of paper, write down a specific statement about what you're after. If you're looking for several different things, write each one of them down in a separate paragraph. As you find the answer to each item you're seeking, cross it off your list.

IDENTIFY YOUR SOURCES

At the beginning of your research, you'll want to think about where you might find the information you need. You're interested, naturally, in doing the job as quickly as possible, so you'll want to line up the prospectively most productive resources. Think about these:

People

People are usually a good resource because even if they don't know the specific facts you want, they may be able to tell you where to go to get the facts. Therefore, draw up a list of people who might help you.

It will speed up your research if you systematize your contacts with them, so that you have a record of what each one told you. For this purpose, you might set up headings like these on a sheet of lined paper:

NAME, ADDRESS, PHONE	POSITION	DATE CONTACTED	RECOMMENDATIONS

Under "Recommendations," you'll put down any comments that the person made which might be helpful. If the person suggests other people to contact, add their names to your list. If the person suggests other resources, such as books or records, write them down here, as well as on a separate sheet of paper. Head the paper with an appropriate headline on it such as, "Books to Research."

Company Records

Your company may have much of the information you're looking for in its records. Think about what records might contain it, and make a note of them. And this is one of the questions you can raise when you contact people: "Do you know of any company records that might have the information I'm seeking?"

Libraries

Your local library may be able to provide you with the information you need. Describe what you're looking for in broad terms so that the librarian can offer the greatest possible number of suggestions.

In addition to your local library, you might want to check specialized libraries. There are many different kinds. For example:

Association libraries. Many professional and trade associations maintain libraries of specialized material.

Company libraries. Your own company or suppliers, customers, and competitors may have libraries of specialized material which may provide you with information.

School libraries. Colleges and universities in your area often have specialized collections; they may have the information you want.

Public Relations Departments

Most larger companies have public relations departments, which frequently can give you a substantial amount of material about their company and—less often—about their industry. As a general rule, the larger the company, the more information their P.R. department will be able to offer. If you don't know whom to contact, a telephone call or letter to the Director of Public Relations at the company's headquarters will usually bring a response.

Associations

There are tens of thousands of trade and professional associations with vast quantities of information in their files. Your public library can provide you with directories that will give you the names and addresses of associations that may be helpful to you. Often, the directories will give you the name of the chief officers, so you can figure out whom to contact.

Government Printing Office

The U.S. Government Printing Office publishes books and brochures on an incredibly wide variety of subjects. To find out what the Office might have that would be useful, write them a letter describing your project and the kinds of information you're looking for. They'll probably respond with a great deal that's irrelevant and a few things that are priceless. Write: Superintendent of Documents, Government Printing Office, Washington, D.C. 20402.

KEEPING RECORDS

You'll save a lot of time if you keep careful files right from the start instead of waiting until your information piles up in a hopeless swirl of tilting stacks of paper. Most professional researchers use two simple tools for organizing their information: the index card and the file folder.

Index Cards

The two popular index card sizes are 3×5 and 4×6. While the smaller size is more convenient to carry in your pocket, the larger size holds more information. You may want them lined on one side or blank, but the lines may help you to write more neatly.

Index cards provide a superb way to collect and organize small pieces of information. However, it's very important to put a headline at the top of each card, so that you can file it and retrieve it when you want it. Usually, subject headings are the most convenient: one or two words describing the subject of the material on the card. If you're collecting a lot of cards, you may want to store them in an index card file, which you can get from a stationery store; and you may find it convenient to buy a set of tab cards. They come in many styles: blank; with letters, numbers, or dates; or with other kinds of information.

File Folders

You'll need file folders if your research project involves the collection of anything larger than an index card. Find a drawer to store them in. If you start out by stacking them on shelves or in odd corners, you'll soon find yourself wasting an enormous amount of time looking for what you want. As with index cards, put a meaningful subject heading on the tab of each folder. Also, as an aid in keeping your files neat, write on each document the name of the folder in which you place it. That way, when you replace it, you'll know immediately where it's supposed to go.

─────────────── **HELPFUL HINT** ───────────────

Remember your sources. Whenever you've finished writing any information on an index card, be sure to write down where it came from: get the name of the person if it's from a conversation. If it's from a written source, write its title and page number. If you're going to give full credit to this source when your information is printed, also write down the name of the publisher and the publication date.

HELPFUL REFERENCE VOLUMES

Information About Corporations

The Fortune Directory
Moody's Manual of Investments
Standard Corporation Records
Thomas's Register of American Manufacturers

Bibliographies of Business Information

Comans, E. T., Jr. *Sources of Business Information.* University of California Press, Berkeley.

Johnson, H. W. *How to Use the Business Library.* South-Western Publishing Co., Cincinnati.

Management Information Guide Series. Gate Publishing Co., Detroit.

Public Affairs Information Service Bulletins.

Statistical Guides

Business Cycle Developments. U.S. Bureau of the Census, Monthly.

Federal Reserve Bulletin. U.S. Board of Governors of the Federal Reserve System, Monthly.

Handbook of Basic Economic Statistics. Economics Statistics Bureau, Washington, D.C., Monthly.

Monthly Labor Review, U.S. Bureau of Labor Statistics.

Statistical Abstract of the United States. U.S. Bureau of the Census.

Survey of Current Business. U.S. Department of Commerce, Monthly.

General Information

Business Periodical Index
Economic Almanac
Encyclopaedia Britannica
New York Times Index
Reader's Guide to Periodical Literature
Wall Street Journal Index
Who's Who in America

Index